THE CoacH

Creating Partnerships for a Competitive Edge

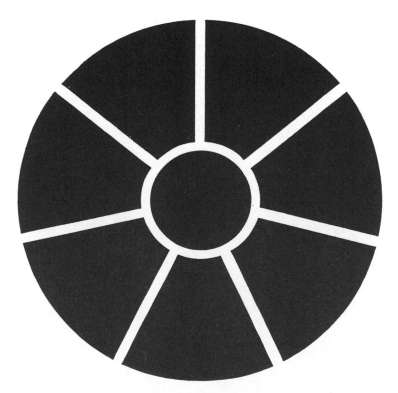

PUBLISHED BY THE CENTER FOR MANAGEMENT
AND ORGANIZATION EFFECTIVENESS

CMOE

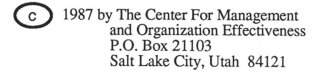
Tenth Printing, April 1992

ACKNOWLEDGEMENT

We would like to express our deep appreciation for the support of those who encouraged, inspired, and assisted us over the last ten years, as this book became a reality.

Dr. Oakley Gordon and Linda Kruse were responsible for creating opportunities that made the research and data gathering possible. Dr. Toby Lafferty, Helen Hodgson, Debbie Stowell, and Karen Okawa played central roles in fine tuning, producing and editing the manuscript. They were patient with our imperfections and worked hard to meet the deadlines.

Roy Yamahiro and Pete Block provided support and conceptual inspiration that has helped shape and influence our thinking about leadership in a positive and constructive way. An additional thanks to all of those in the client organizations that we have worked with to train managers around the coaching skills. Their confidence, feedback, and patience to stay with us during the years of refinement and improvement on the coaching model have been deeply appreciated. We hope these clients and future clients will enjoy the direction and depth of this material.

Lastly to Debbie Stowell, Judy Starcevich, and our families--their constant support and assistance have made our efforts enjoyable.

THE *CoacH*

Creating Partnerships
for a
Competitive Edge

Steven J.
Stowell, Ph.D.

Matt M.
Starcevich, Ph.D.

The Center For Management and Organization Effectiveness

P.O. Box 21103
Salt Lake City, Utah 84121
(801) 943-6310

P.O. Box 2505
Bartlesville, Okla. 74006
(918) 333-6609

CMOE PRESENTS

THE FIRST IN A SERIES ON

PARTNERSHIPS IN THE WORK PLACE

THE CENTER FOR MANAGEMENT AND ORGANIZATION EFFECTIVENESS (CMOE)

Organized in 1979 with the following mission:

1. To provide training for managers and employees.
2. To solve difficult organization problems.
3. To design and implement quality human resource systems.
4. To conduct practical and useful organization research.
5. To publish the results of our work.

Our staff all hold advanced degrees in the behavioral sciences and are consulting with many of the Fortune 500 firms to improve management and organization effectiveness.

TABLE OF CONTENTS

CHAPTER 1

ABOUT THIS BOOK

A. OUR PROMISE:
WHY YOU SHOULD READ THIS BOOK

There is no question that the role of the leader will be different in the future, different because of technological advances, increased competition (both domestic and international), and the desire of employees to be more involved in managing their own work. Leaders will need to instill a new competitive spirit in employees to streamline work, reduce errors, respond to customer needs, and solve challenging problems. *People* will have the greatest influence on productivity, excellence, and quality, if leaders can empower employees and give them more autonomy while maintaining *effective accountability*. This will mean a substantial change in the role of the traditional leader and his/her skills to interact on a one-to-one basis. The new job of the leader will be to *coach*, develop, train, delegate, facilitate, and run interference--rather than doing all the planning, organizing, and directing from an authoritative base.

New Age of Leadership

To Coach

In the future, leaders will be dealing with a more educated, talented group of employees who have definite interests and aspirations. Leaders and employees are becoming more like partners whose common cause is to accomplish the job in the best way possible. Because organizations have limited resources and because actions that can be undertaken are limited, leaders and employees will need to develop a common vision or mission of the work to be done. Leaders will then coach, monitor, and help employees fulfill that

Develop a common vision

1

vision and purpose. Leaders must learn how to turn employees into allies, not adversaries, without sacrificing standards of quality and productivity. In fact, the main reasons we advocate coaching are because it enables us to more adequately respond to the demands of customers, maintain standards, and fulfill the purpose of existing in the organization.

Some leaders may find this new approach to leadership challenging because their own bosses may not be the best models to follow. In the past we have looked at employees as children needing a benevolent dictator rather than as entrepreneurial partners. More and more employees now want to be included, to contribute, and to be treated as adults, not like just extra pairs of hands or pack mules. This new attitude will test the patience, skills, and knowledge of leaders.

Our Promise

So this book is about your beliefs as a leader regarding your employees and how they should be managed and directed in a very positive way. Our promise to you is that if you will seriously ponder the message of this book, begin practicing the behaviors, and assimilate the values advocated, you will definitely succeed in winning the cooperation and support of employees. It won't come overnight, and you will find some employees who defy the recommendations that we suggest. These exceptions will require a different and perhaps traditional management style. However, others will appreciate the refreshing difference in your approach and will reward you with incomparable levels of performance. We also promise to try to make the reading and search for solutions interesting and to the point.

CHAPTER 1

ABOUT THIS BOOK

So there you have it. There are many books on leadership you can choose to read. Choose this book if you want to concentrate on specifics related to positive leadership skills and coaching interaction skills. We believe coaching is a constructive game for leaders to learn. There are a lot of games to learn; some good, some not. Why not learn the art of a good one?

If you want specific leadership skills

B. GUIDE TO THIS BOOK

Not everyone likes to read a book from cover to cover. For those who like to pick and choose, here is a brief guide for your travel.

Chapter 1

Chapter One, Partnerships are Everywhere, is a statement of what we are advocating for future leader-employee relationships. Coaching plays a central role in creating and maintaining partner oriented relationships.

Chapter 2

Chapter Two, Memories Never Die, is an intriguing story about a manager faced with a challenging coaching opportunity. As the story unfolds, the manager encounters obstacles and then discovers the actions that are needed to be a successful coach.

Chapter 3

Chapter Three, The 8-Step Model, is a summary discussion of behaviors that we discovered from our study of effective coaches. This model represents a road map for holding a successful coaching meeting.

Chapter 4

Chapter Four, Supporting Skills, represents the skills that make the 8-Step Model a positive and collaborative experience for the leader and employee. This chapter contains specific hints for the manager to follow when using the 8-Step Model.

Chapter 5

Chapter Five, The Coach's Contribution, explores a range of potential problems the manager must plan for. The manager's response to these issues will determine how he/she will approach and orchestrate the coaching meeting

4

CHAPTER 1

ABOUT THIS BOOK

Chapter Six, Positive Motivational Coaching, takes the 8-Step Model beyond working with specific problems to coaching the above average performer or the employee who has no performance problem but needs a challenge or more job satisfaction in order to contribute to the organization.

Chapter 6

Chapter Seven, Concluding Thoughts, presents a number of ideas that help put the entire coaching process into perspective (Beyond Coaching, Group Problem Solving, etc.). Look at these as bonus ideas to help make what you have learned even more effective.

Chapter 7

In the Appendices, you will find a Planning Guide for the Coaching Session and a Summary of the Training Design we have used to teach these concepts and skills to thousands of managers. You will also find a form for your convenience in ordering additional copies of this book.

The Appendices

We hope this guide will help in making your reading more enjoyable and productive for you--let's get started.

C. PARTNERSHIPS ARE EVERYWHERE

Leaders are partners first

You hear a lot about partnerships in life--in marriages, businesses, tennis or bridge. There are investment partnerships, limited partnerships, law or C.P.A. partnerships; in short, the term partnership is applied to relationships in many facets of our experience. It usually creates positive visions and feelings within us, and coaching is essentially building a meaningful partnership with employees. We believe that the role of leaders and partners should be fused: great leaders must be partners first. Increasingly, workers are adopting the philosophy that the only authority deserving of loyalty and allegiance is that which is freely granted by the employee.

Definition

Webster defines a partner as an ally or an association built around common interests and goals. The concept denotes cooperation in a joint venture or challenge. A partnership is a relationship that emphasizes equal status (rather than inequality) and encompasses a certain independence as well as certain obligations and commitments. Partnerships usually require direct interaction and contact. A good partnership is like a good contract: It requires mutual consent, valid consideration from both parties, and willingness to respond to the other's highest-level needs first.

We are strong advocates of partnerships because leaders and employees have more significant commonalities than differences.

CHAPTER 1

ABOUT THIS BOOK

Leader-Employee Commonalities tend to be significant:

• Both have a lot to gain if the parties succeed in the job.

• Both have their careers and mortgages on the line if they fail in the job.

• Both have to be concerned about the efficient use of resources.

• Both have to take risks in order to survive and prosper in challenging environments.

Leader-Employee Differences tend to be minor:

• The job title is a little different.

• The leader's box on the organization chart is 1/4 inch higher on the page.

• The leader has a bigger paycheck and bigger mortgage.

• The leader gets chewed out first and the employee second if the unit fails on assignments.

Partnerships are strengthened through positive motivational coaching as well as honest problem-solving coaching. Coaching is the most useful tool in building "master" partnerships with each employee on a one-to-one basis. In essence, partnerships are a way of achieving a mature, adult-to-adult, relationship with employees.

**Coaching :
a tool
for building
partnerships**

Good coaching depends on good leaders, and leadership is a unique phenomenon in any organization. It is unique because the corporation can more easily control other elements of the business than it can the quality of leadership and partnerships. Leadership is elusive, and is mainly up to you individually and what you want to make of it.

It's in your control

As a leader, it is within your control. You largely determine the quality of relationships despite any rules and policies of the company that encourage quality leadership. The fact of the matter is, poor leaders can hide behind "busy work" and activities. The decision is yours.

Organizations need leaders who have personal commitment to the idea of building partnerships with employees. Sure it is easier said than done--especially when others who have influence and occupy leadership positions above yours are not as concerned and interested in building partnerships as you are. Usually when we bring up this topic with groups, everyone nods and says, "Right on." The only problem is you are working with the wrong group. You need to work with higher management or lower management, or the personnel people--then they supply some group other than themselves. When we work with these other groups, they say the same thing. . .so far we haven't been able to find the right group yet who needs this stuff.

8

CHAPTER 1

ABOUT THIS BOOK

The reality for most organizations is that great leadership at the working level is still largely wishful thinking, often seen as a luxury that can't be afforded. Our position is that we can't wait until we can afford good leadership in today's competitive environment. The problem is that when cash is tight, most firms are willing to "mortgage their future" and save a few dollars by cutting their leadership development efforts, throwing espoused leadership principles out the window, and reverting to "tough tactics" with employees. And many individual managers know that as long as they keep their heads down and look busy no one will bug them about stuff like "partnerships." Furthermore, a good working manager usually has a hard time breaking away from the press of the daily routine. . .we believe the activity trap is literally addictive and keeps leaders away from partnership building. Daily routine demands push leaders into doing things right (details), rather than doing the right things (concentrating on really important tasks).

Let's face it. A lot of worthy *activities* that need to get done fly in the face of making *leadership and people* number 1 in the corporation. Our best assessment is that in most organizations people are number 7 on the priority list and moving up slowly.

Our feeling is we ought to be glad that people are not number 1, because it adds some meaning to the job of leadership and gives us something to do and work for. Somehow leaders have to learn to be more effective at balancing and shifting from *activities* to serious leadership.

It's leadership not activity

As much value needs to be put on excellence in leadership as on excellence in managing activities (like having a clean desk, filling out time cards, and checking reports). We have to get away from the notion that to further your career ambitions, you need only manage activities well. Leaders need to concentrate more on effective leadership *right where they are* and not worry about trying to look good on the surface for the sake of a little upward mobility.

The task

The task of the "leader/partner" is to establish goals and missions, to listen, to be accessible and understanding, to empower others, and to maintain accountability. Leaders need foresight and must build their organization into a productive community. They need to have a sense of unlimited liability for their employees' productivity and development and to display unconditional support and concern.

We've never had it!!

Our contention and central point is that leader/employee partnerships are in trouble. Actually, if you take an objective look at the situation, leader/employee partnerships have never been out of trouble in American industry. Our feeling is that American industry has never really discovered the power and benefits of really strong, meaningful leader/employee partnerships in the work place. Traditionally, leaders and employees have acted more like adversaries than like partners. Relationships of the past have been marked by cautiousness, some secretiveness, high authority, and heavy control. The goal of the coaching process is to create *durable* partnerships that can easily

10

withstand the stress and agonies of problem solving and the joys and benefits of positive and motivational coaching. Accepting an employee as a partner means the leader respects his/her stewardship, honors the rights of the employee, and in a business sense uses the human resource effectively by taking full advantage of its wisdom, skills, and potential. A leader becomes not a critic, but rather a coach and helper. Oftentimes leaders want to coach an employee but come off sounding like a critic who just wasted an evening at the opening of a mediocre Broadway musical. In either situation, the reviews are particularly painful for those involved. They tear you down and affect your self-esteem and self-worth. The leader as a coach must try hard to avoid this type of confrontation the way a leader views employees or the status given them in the mind of the leader will probably be reflected in the way they are treated in a coaching discussion.

Concentrating on leadership means that you need to make some very clear conscious choices about the types or forms of partnerships you want to create with your employees. Like it or not, either productive or counterproductive partnerships will emerge. Our feeling is that leaders can take an active role in shaping and building the kind of partnerships they want. The choice boils down to a selection from four basic types.

What form of partnership do you want?

The first type of partnership is steeped in American history, and particularly in the history of the industrial revolution. It is also the partnership model used by the military

1-Adversarial

(quite successfully in some situations). We believe this "adversarial model of partnerships" motivates workers to seek the help of unions and third-party representation. Historically, leaders of profit-motivated organizations harbored these assumptions about their employee partners. "Employees are lazy, greedy, and stupid. Consequently we will pay them only for the work they do, we won't trust them with responsibility, we will design their jobs so simply that monkeys could handle them, and we will keep tight control on them." People were viewed as just another resource, like equipment and buildings; they were taught not to think but simply to submit to authority. What does this approach do to the attitude of your employee partners? They resent it and are bored by their work. They become cautious and overly dependent on leaders for every instruction. Because they are not empowered to do anything on their own, they feel confined and relate the organization to a penal institution. Leaders are perceived as bosses and bullies. We even have a hard time suggesting that this is a form of partnership. But it exists today, too much of it in fact. This approach has been hard to eliminate because in an earlier time it worked. It helped make America great and so a lot of people who are resistant to change have adopted an attitude of "Why knock it?"

2-Patriarch/ Matriarch

The next type of partnership is born out of family and parental experiences, the "patriarchal partnership." Here the leader plays the role of father or mother. It is different from the adversarial partnerships in that the parent means well, wants the best for the employee, and wants to

12

provide protection. The relationship is seductive and feels good. In this partnership, if the employees keep their heads down and don't ask a lot of questions, they assume they will get ahead and things will work out. This partnership causes employees to feel and act like children. Risk taking is not encouraged. The employees can take comfort in the fact that nothing will ever be their fault. Everything can always be blamed on the leader. As employees, approval is sought from Dad or Mom. This partnership rests on accountability and control, but includes very little autonomy to stretch, to be innovative, or to grow in abilities and talent. Employees are robbed of their aspirations, dreams, and self-confidence.

The next type of partnership is the silent partnership which unfortunately is far too common in industry today. The silent partnership is born out of leader apathy and benign neglect. We see a lot of working managers who are willing to accept whatever level of performance they happen to get from their employees. Sometimes these working managers just don't appear to notice or observe what is really going on in their organization. At times they seem inattentive and even disinterested in employee behavior and good leadership. Other silent leaders more consciously abdicate their leadership responsibilities because they don't like meaningful leadership tasks and get more satisfaction from being busy doing their own thing. Whether the apathy and silence are intentional or not, the result is the same: employees feel unchallenged, neglected, and unappreciated. They don't grow and learn from your experience and knowledge. This

3-Silent

style of partnership is a mixed blessing. The good news is employees have a lot of autonomy, and that's great if all of your employees are talented self-starters. In fact, being a leader would be simple if you had perfect people; however, the imperfections in employees give the job of leader its meaning. The bad news about the silent leader is the lack of controls and little accountability. Silent partnerships do not work because whatever success your unit achieves will result from the behavior of those who work for you. You can't be passive and content; you have to be an active force for setting the direction, improving and shaping the efforts of your employees.

4-Entrepreneurial

The fourth type of partnership, born out of the need to have a strong *competitive* unit, is what we call the "entrepreneurial partnership." The leader in this partnership maintains high accountability and high autonomy. The partnership requires serious collaboration and *coaching* from the leader. Regular interactions have purpose and meaning. Problems are confronted in a supportive fashion, and successes are acknowledged and reinforced. The leader-employee pair works and collaborates in an effort to do whatever is necessary to see that each other's performance is maximized and that the unit functions efficiently. It is no different from any other type of successful partnership in life. However, the organizational pyramid or hierarchy and the risk of learning to trust others unfortunately force some distortion in potentially good partnerships. An entrepreneurial partnership feels different; it creates doubts and goes against the traditional grain of organizations.

CHAPTER 1

ABOUT THIS BOOK

At first it feels a little bit intimidating and threatening to work with employees who are empowered as partners. Moving to the more ideal entrepreneurial partnership means that you are choosing:

It means

- to be an architect of your unit vs. another laborer or expert

- to be a resource or helper vs. an obstacle or constraint

- to be open with information vs. closed

- to value accountability and results vs. control and rules

- to value autonomy and risk taking vs. dependency and cautiousness

- to see your unit become competitive and great rather than achieve personal fame and visibility

- to be direct and authentic with employees vs. indirect and manipulative

- to be a coach and problem solver vs. a criticizer and complainer

These statements represent the vision of the entrepreneurial partnership. The *way to move closer* to achieving the entrepreneurial partnership is through *regular contact and coaching*. Coaching is the key mechanism for partnership building and maintenance. It gives you the opportunity to change and focus behavior that concerns you, or to motivate and reinforce behavior that you find desirable. Each coaching session is the

Through regular contact and coaching

ultimate stage for acting out the type of partnership that you want to create.

Partner-oriented mentality views employees as equals with a lot at stake in the work place. Employees who are able and want to contribute and those who are close to and familiar with the work should have the opportunity. Employees who can't currently contribute to the partnership or to the resolution of job challenges and problems, need to be brought along more slowly. If they choose not to participate, you need to say goodbye to them compassionately and gracefully.

Not all employees want, nor do they deserve, partnership status. Some employees treat the leader and the job as mechanically as some leaders treat employees. However, we believe that the leader is responsible for initiating a change in the nature of the relationship and communicating the concepts of partnership and what it means to the employees. It is a key leadership responsibility to coach, train, and develop employees--and this is one major distinguishing feature of the leader's role as compared to the employee's.

What effective leaders do

Through 10 years of research and observation, we have found that skillful leaders rely less on authority and dictums and more on collaboration and negotiation. Effective leaders use their ability to reason, to ask penetrating questions, and to listen, rather than relying on the official authority of their position. Finally, we have noticed that effective leaders can blend and weave ideas and solutions and that they defer to the

CHAPTER 1

ABOUT THIS BOOK

employee when appropriate. If you push, hammer, and require employees, who are potential partners and allies, to work in a bent-over position, they naturally become angry and withdraw their valuable support and cooperation. Although they will perform according to your wishes as long as you watch over them, you will have created conflict and resentment--that has a nasty and lasting emotional effect. The result is usually an erosion of trust which requires time and a lot of good-faith actions to restore. If you push people around and act like "king of the hill," employees will respond by acting and thinking like gofers.

"Great leaders try to understand before they expect to be understood."

In developing a partnership with your employees, you are aiding them in achieving their potential. The key to success is pulling together and teamwork. The better one partner looks, the better the other one will too. The fundamental goal and underlying premise of any coaching discussion or intervention is always mutual benefit.

The key is teamwork

A lot of power and creativity can come from building and maintaining a good partnership. Those of us who have been in one can vouch for this from first-hand experience. Partnerships don't always guarantee that times will be easy, but they do mean the difficult times and problems can be overcome and solved. It requires a lot of candor, skill, and courage to talk straight to your partner (be it employee, spouse, or investor). Leaders must find space in their busy days to create positive partnerships with their employees. That's what this book is all about. We hope you will enjoy reading about the coaching process and how it can be the

ENTREPRENEURIAL PARTNERSHIPS

That's what this book is all about

17

key to creating an "entrepreneurial" partnership.

CHAPTER 2

MEMORIES NEVER DIE

"You're not going to like what I've got to say, and I don't want you to blame me for this, but management feels it's best for you to speak to Pat directly. Since she'll be returning to your department, you can make the chain of command clear to her from the beginning." Fred's news totally ruined my day. I swallowed my resentment but couldn't help thinking, "Why can't you talk to her? I didn't make the decision to put her back into my department." The whole fiasco was an incredible turn of events.

I can still look back two years ago and remember Pat's first day on the job after I hired her. She was determined to do well, eager to please, and appeared to want to get ahead. But most of all, I was struck by her attractiveness and irresistible social skills. As time passed, it became increasingly obvious that her presence in my department was a mixed blessing. I couldn't help liking her. She was bright and learned fast, maybe too fast. Family problems had forced her to drop out of college after completing three years towards a Bachelor's degree in business, but she had immediately enrolled in night school and was well on her way to finishing her degree. At 28, Pat showed occasional signs of brilliance and the potential to mature into a highly valued employee. When I had needed her help most, she came through with creative solutions to problems and willingly worked overtime to see them become reality.

Pat's past

I felt that she had the ability to go a long way in this organization, so it bothered me when I began to see the limitations. Rumors began to circulate about her, minimal at first, that she would use any means available to

19

advance her career. In important but subtle ways, she *wasn't* fitting into the culture of this organization. Relationships with co-workers might be O.K. in other organizations, but not in this archaic institution.

I felt that I was on the firing line. She had so many strengths--I could see those--but a less rational instinct warned me that she was cunning and deceptive, perhaps willing to put her own needs above the best interests of the company. I became increasingly torn about her value as an employee and finally called her in to discuss my concern. "Pat, I want you to know first that I value your work and I have no desire to limit your personal freedoms, but please don't let your own objectives interfere with the ability of other employees to do their jobs. And the same holds true with our customers; they can't be compromised." I'll never forget the look of deep and genuine hurt that Pat couldn't hide, but her response was professional.

"I had no idea that you were thinking those things about me. I'm glad you spoke to me. I'll really pay more attention to what I'm doing. I don't want to be misunderstood. You've got to know that I want what is best for the company as well as for my own career."

She sounded so sincere that day we talked it was no wonder that I was disappointed when her actions seemed to belie her words.

And along comes Bob

I have to admit that Pat wasn't the only one swept off her feet by Bob. He was appointed the new Director of Sales and Marketing about six months after Pat began working

20

with my department. Bob was a highly capable individual, and I admired him as well. He had the rare combination of hard driving intensity coupled with a deep concern for people. Customers were a priority for him. He'd push the staff to work long hours,to have projects completed on time. He wasn't always popular in that regard. He always maintained a personal contact with customers, as well as staff, from the beginning to the end of even the smallest job. It was no wonder that he was known for his ability to create new markets for the company's services. On the other hand, some people saw Bob as using his personality and charisma to pull him through on big deals and, I must admit, he struck me as something of the flamboyant, high roller type.

It made sense that Bob liked working with Pat. Whenever projects involved both of our departments, they'd come back from lunch brimming with energy, new ideas, and plans, when most of the staff was content to relax after too satisfying a lunch. It was their combined energy that propelled the office on the big and more difficult projects.

That was when the rumors intensified. At first it seemed petty--the references to long lunches or weekends spent in the office together working on projects, but I began to notice things too. The casual lunches developed into lengthier ones and soon an afternoon off now and then. That was when I became alarmed and decided to talk to her again. I could see the effects on the morale of the team.

What's going on?

"Pat, look. . . you're an adult, I can't tell you what to do with your personal life. But I am concerned about the level of teamwork and the reputation our entire department is getting. I don't want you to get hurt in this situation. I've seen too many people end up holding the bag." I must admit that I found it painfully difficult to confront an employee who was basically good and had a lot of potential. My feeling reminded me of a favorite quotation mounted on my office wall:

> "COACHING IS THE MOST UNCOMFORTABLE, AVOIDED, AND MISHANDLED OF ALL MANAGEMENT TASKS."

Pat's promotion

I guess things happened faster than even I had imagined. Pat's promotion was very much on the "Q.T." Her position wasn't even posted for people to bid on. In fact, the way I heard about it was a "Post-It-Note" on my door from Bob, the Marketing Director, informing me that Pat had been promoted to the position of Senior Client Sales Representative in his division. I couldn't have been happier myself. I was ecstatic. A nasty problem had been plucked off my back, and Bob and Pat were no longer my concern. By this time, rumors about their affair were out in the open, although they seemed to work harder and pretended that nothing was going on. It was no secret that Bob always closed the door when he had individual consultations with Pat. He never made that a practice with the other sales reps. I can tell you one thing for sure; Bob's boss wasn't about to confront him. After all, Bob was delivering exactly what he had been hired to. Bob had been working with the company for over a year when management intervened. It was all pretty hush, hush at first, until the facts gradually came to light about Bob and his manipulative style. Rumors were rampant about how Bob had overstepped his approval of authority on some major deals and then, to top it off, I think that management got a little tired of Bob's expense account. More and more Bob wanted to play this game according to his rules, and I think top management was getting a little tired and felt threatened by Bob's success. From that point on, the stories got a little weird. All anyone knows for certain is that Bob was in his office the next day, packing up his personal belongings. The official announcement from the C.E.O. was curt: "Due to alternative career interests, the Director of Sales and Marketing has elected to pursue other career options and his resignation has been regretfully accepted. I hope you will join with me in wishing Bob the best of luck in his new endeavors in the Yukon." Not a bad coverup if the rumors hadn't circulated so quickly. As it turned out, the C.E.O. would have been better off if he had just leveled with everyone about why Bob was fired.

As far as I am concerned, it doesn't make a lot of difference what happened to Bob and Pat. The bottom line is that now I have to handle the whole messy situation and at this point, it's hard for me to remember anything good about Pat. One thing is certain. She won't take a demotion and pay cut lying down. I don't know which I dreaded worse-- telling her or my department.

Bob's luck ends

Pat's demotion

People were resentful when she was promoted so quickly. Her new job had been exciting--much more than the one that she left. It would be painful to come back to a job with so much less potential and prestige, not to mention the cut in pay, and work with people who would have to be laughing at her.

Why me?

As I drove home, I tried to sort through all my thoughts and feelings. Why is this such a problem for me? For the most part I am a pretty good manager. I try hard, and I have been with the organization eight years. I think most of my people would rate me as a good leader. I try to stay up on management articles, and I attend at least one workshop each year to be prepared for situations like this. Like most managers I am faced with a lot of time pressures, and I feel caught in the middle of daily routines and activities. I probably spend too much time making sure everything is done right, the details, and not enough time on doing the things that matter more in the long run. I tell everyone that I have one of the best groups of employees that a manager could ask for. But I have to admit that, when it comes right down to it, I see things every day that could be done differently and more effectively.

Pat isn't the only one who could use a little more attention from me. Frankly, if I had my choice, I would much rather do other things than confront employees about things that need attention or improvement. Besides, I don't think they gave me this manager's job because of my proven leadership skills. I was promoted because I was a damn good technician, because I got my monthly reports in on time, and because I completed my projects under budget. Even when I try to put in ten-hour days, it still seems like my leadership responsibilities suffer. You know, maybe that's why I am putting in ten-hour days; maybe I am doing a lot of work that belongs to others, and there isn't enough teamwork in the department. With any other group of employees I would probably be putting in seven-or eight-hour days. . . . But why does it seem like it's always me who gets to handle these miserable situations like the one with Pat?

I had little appetite for dinner, and could tell it was going to be one of those nights. I finally retreated to my den and reached for my journal to make my routine daily entries. This journal preserves much that I learned in trying to help Pat weather a major crisis in her professional life. In hopes that these concepts might also be of use to you, the reader, the relevant entries accompany my story.

As I picked up the pencil, I could feel the tenseness as my grip tightened. I had a hard time recalling anything about my day except the anger and resentment caused by the predicament with Pat. I wanted to remind her about all her mistakes, what they were costing, and how they had put her career in a hole. For some reason I had backed off these negative emotions, maybe because I tried putting myself into her shoes.

MY

JOURNAL

NEGATIVE EMOTIONS CREATE NEGATIVE ACTIONS AND REACTIONS

As I reflected on situations with other employees, I could envision how a positive mind set had helped me, and how painfully long it had taken me before I realized it. Like it or not, my attitude would play just as important a role in resolution of this issue. I started to think about why and how Pat had gotten into a mess so contrary to my wishes and the culture of the organization. The more I tried to make sense out of this, the less I could. I asked myself whether it was important to understand why, or whether I should accept the situation as a 'fait accompli.' What I realized was that Pat needed a manager who wouldn't exacerbate her painful rejection.

I DON'T HAVE TO UNDERSTAND WHY IN ORDER TO BE HELPFUL

That realization helped to relax the confusion I felt. I began to focus more on the end result I wanted from this situation. I didn't want to get aggressive with Pat, yet it seemed like a disservice to withhold information. Could she be expected to change if she didn't have a clear picture of the situation? I felt torn; I wanted to be nice as well as honest. The manager I admired most in life had that very impressive ability.

26

Having worked through my approach, I was beginning to feel better. This felt like the type of role I wanted to play. I went to bed thinking that I had the situation under control. I would meet with Pat the next day, break the news to her, and then wait exactly one week for things to settle down before I met with Pat again. There was no doubt in my mind that we would have lots to talk about after a week back in my department. I slipped my pocket calendar from my briefcase and made a commitment: a second meeting with Pat at 11:30 a.m., one week from the initial meeting.

My carefully reasoned analysis of the situation and my optimism about facing Pat had vanished by the next morning. I awoke with a clear sense of impending doom and was praying for a miracle. But when neither the Good Witch of the North nor the Blue Fairy appeared, I resigned myself to the meeting.

Once I accepted the inevitable, I decided that I might as well get it over with. I headed for Pat's office as soon as I arrived at work. One look at her, and I knew that bringing her back into the department was not going to be

PEOPLE APPRECIATE AN HONEST CONFRONTATION AS LONG AS THEY DON'T FEEL PUNISHED IN THE PROCESS

FRIDAY APRIL 2

**1st discussion
with Pat**

27

easy. She greeted me with a mixture of relief and hostility. I didn't waste any time. I said, "Pat, I'm sure you've been wondering how you would be affected now that Bob has left the company. I don't know if you'll like this a whole lot, but management has decided to reassign you to your old job in my department."

Pat went white. It was clear that this was not what she had been expecting. "I don't believe it, that's not fair! I'm being discriminated against! That's insane, I'll file a complaint."

Her anger was so apparent that I felt myself getting defensive and wanting to argue back. Knowing that wouldn't help, I asked her to consider the situation more realistically. "Weren't you using Bob for your own ends, just as he was using you?"

"Fireworks"

"So you believe the rumors too! I work hard at my job. I was promoted because of the work I've done and my abilities--*not* my relationship with Bob. Now what will people be saying? How in the world do you expect me to face the people in that department?"

When she had calmed down a little, I explained how we would bring her back into the department and what my expectations were. I reminded her of the problems that I noticed before she was promoted and made clear that certain standards would have to be met.

Despite Pat's anger, disappointment, and now unnerving silence, I tried to convince myself

CHAPTER 2

MEMORIES NEVER DIE

that she would cooperate. What other choice did she have? She's pulled through before. I left her office with a cautious optimism that things would work out. There was even a sense of relief. . . giving her the bad news was behind me.

The next few days revealed that any optimism was premature. The effect that Pat was having on the department was decidedly negative. She became resentful and defensive, and people were rapidly getting tired of it. To make matters worse, she seemed to be intentionally sabotaging the work of the department in an effort to get even. People were becoming increasingly angry, and I feared open revolt. It made me question my leadership skills. Why was I letting this situation get out of control? Did Pat really have a potential that was worth trying to protect and foster? What could I do or say that would let her know I understood how angry and hurt she was and, at the same time, motivate her to see her experience with Bob as something she had learned from and moved beyond?

Pat's performance deteriorates

Pat was losing the respect of her colleagues, what little she had left. Few of them had seen her tremendous creativity, her ability to produce under pressure. I often wished that I hadn't either. Firing her would be painful, but, on the plus side, termination would be a quick and permanent solution. Instead I was torn between that alternative and trying to salvage the situation. Maybe I wasn't capable of turning this around, but then this would be my failure as well as hers. I wasn't quite ready to admit defeat.

THE COACH

MONDAY APRIL 5

I had put a busy week behind me, the problem with Pat pushed out of mind by immediate office demands. Monday started out wonderfully! I woke up early, had time for a leisurely jog, and even spent twenty minutes in my den reviewing files and preparing for a luncheon meeting with my boss and some new managers. As I do every morning, I checked my calendar book. Suddenly I stared at my handwriting. It seemed almost to reach out and choke me. No matter how I tried, I couldn't deny that I had written the words, *"11:30 a.m. consultation with Pat."* I really didn't need this. Why did it have to be today? I wildly considered alternatives, but none of them worked. My mind was reeling with anxiety. I was trying to think fast. There must be some way to escape from my commitment to work with Pat. Then I stopped, as I realized my motives. "What am I doing? Am I running away from this?"

I even remember reading that employees are more willing to get feedback than leaders are willing to give it. I recommitted to myself that I would not fall into the avoidance trap or take the easy way out. Besides, I knew my boss would call me before 12:00 for the luncheon meeting we had with the new managers. I figured I could "gut" it out for 20 or 30 minutes and then I would be rescued.

CONSTRUCTIVE
OPENNESS
WITH EMPLOYEES
TAKES A LOT
OF
LEADERSHIP
COURAGE !!

30

CHAPTER 2

MEMORIES NEVER DIE

Mornings pass quickly when the worst is ahead. It seemed like 11:30 rolled around like lightning. I hesitated as I picked up the phone and reluctantly dialed Pat's extension. I don't think I have ever talked that fast in my life, but she managed to understand that I was asking her to take a break from her work and join me in my office for a minute.

The atmosphere was icy when she walked in and sat down. I was nervous. The little confidence I had felt a few moments ago drained, leaving an empty feeling in the pit of my stomach. I searched for words, "Can I get you something?" It sounded like I was stalling for time. I closed the door to my office. . .the sound echoed. . .like a vault closing shut. My leg hit the corner of a magazine rack as I headed to safety behind my desk.

2nd discussion with Pat

She sat down. It was hard to make eye contact. The silence was deafening. . . I had to say something. "Uh. . . Pat, do you know why I called you in?" She didn't say anything. That didn't feel like much of a start, but I assumed that she was giving me the green light. "Pat I'm going to get right to the point. I think you have a real attitude problem." Pat rigidly sat up in her chair. She seemed to bristle at this comment. I barged ahead before she could say anything, pointing out that sometimes the truth is painful.

Pat interrupted me and said, "It is not fair. . . it's just not fair." Pat was getting highly emotional, and I could see that my words were cutting pretty deep. I knew I would have to pick up the momentum if we were to make any progress.

Emotions rise

31

"Sometimes life isn't fair. Look, Pat, you have a choice. You can grow up and learn something from this, or you can just run away."

Pat tried to cut in on me. "It's not my fault," she shouted. "It's theirs."

My voice grew stronger. "I don't want to hear about your excuses. I just want to be honest with you, and I want you to be honest with yourself."

"Stop attacking me"

"You've got it all wrong. You have no idea what's been going on. I'm perfectly capable of doing my job. Where do you get off on this anyway? Don't you think it's time for you to stop attacking me? You tell me I can turn over a new leaf, and then you don't give me a chance. I'm sick of it, all of it. . . ."

"Look, Pat, the facts are the facts. You need to quit pouting and take more interest in your work. Everyone in the department has mentioned to me that you're cutting yourself off from the rest of them, and that's creating a communication breakdown that I can't live with!"

Pat responded quickly, "What do you think? Is that how you've seen me acting?"

The silence was deafening.

"Who do you believe? Me or them?"

"Look," I told her, "all I want you to do is stay in the department and try. But look, if things don't change I'll guarantee you it will

CHAPTER 2

MEMORIES NEVER DIE

cost you on your next performance appraisal and on your salary adjustment. I think it's only fair to the rest of the department. Unless you *shape* up, I'll be forced to explore with management the possibility of a transfer into another group where teamwork isn't so critical."

At that, Pat exploded. "If you don't like my work then get rid of me. If communication is what you want, I can handle it, but people in the department better quit treating me like some carnival side show. They better get off my back."

At that moment the phone rang. . . it was my boss saying he was ready for the meeting. I put down the receiver and stood up, "Look, Pat, I didn't want to cut this short, but maybe we shouldn't push this further today. We both need to think about it more before we talk again." It suddenly seemed to be totally out of control, and I pleaded with Pat, "We have to make this thing work. Everyone is watching. Just remember, I hired you. My credibility is on the line too."

Pat just stared at me as if she couldn't believe what she was hearing. "Look, I was promoted because I can handle a challenging job. Just tell me what you want, and leave my personal life and personal choices out of it! They're not your concern. Can't you understand that. . ."

Saved by the bell

"Look, Pat," I interrupted, "let's not blow this out of proportion. I want you to figure out a way to turn this around. . . okay!" By this time I was cramming files into my briefcase like clothes into a suitcase when I am late for a plane. I headed for the door, brushing past her as she stood up. I was walking fast when my thoughts caught up with me.

"Wow, that was close, 20 minutes of pure hell, and it felt like an hour." A little of the tension subsided as I crossed the parking lot. I hated to admit it, but I was relieved that the phone rang. I felt that I was getting nowhere; she just didn't believe me or see that she needed to improve the situation and change her behavior. I wished that there was a way to put up a mirror so that she could see what the rest of the department had been seeing for the past week.

Where did I go wrong?

As I thought back over the way I handled myself at that meeting, I flinched at my own inability to confront her. How could she have discussed or been honest about anything the way I never stopped talking. . . and what was it that she was about to say as I brushed by her at the door?

CHAPTER 2

MEMORIES NEVER DIE

As I joined the others for lunch, I couldn't keep my mind off Pat. If she was responsible for the breakdown in our communication, why was I feeling so bad? Our meeting just hadn't gone the way I had intended.

Lunch with my boss

When my boss asked me to provide some very specific information about how my department could help solve a problem, it was hard to break out of my thoughts. I became confused and had trouble keeping the thread of the discussion. In my fumbling attempt to both disguise and explain my confusion, I began to tell him about the problems with Pat. He was quiet, that confident, unemotional exterior of his emphasizing my agitation. He took off his glasses and methodically rubbed the bridge of his nose. Then he broke in, "We've talked about this type of situation before. You know what top management wants--a smoothly run ship. I can count on you to handle this, can't I?"

"Thanks a lot"

I was fumbling again. "Well sure boss, no problem. You can count on me to straighten Pat out."

"I'm counting on you to keep this from becoming an embarrassment." He put his glasses back on, sat back in his chair, and looked at me. . ."And now we've got some more important issues to cover."

That was definitely the end of that conversation. Great! A little more pressure, just what I needed when I couldn't see my way out of this mess. I sure didn't get any help from my boss on how to best handle Pat.

More pressure

I returned to the office after lunch, dreading the thought that I might run into Pat. I wanted to think through our meeting, but any further exchange with her was not likely to help. I needn't have worried. A note from her was sitting on my desk. "My doctor was able to give me an appointment. I will be gone until morning." What kind of a manager was I? My confidence in my ability to solve this problem was eroding further as I realized that Pat was at least as upset as I was.

Where to turn? I felt like I was rolling down a mountainside with no one to break my fall. Wallowing in self-pity didn't seem like a long-term solution, so I racked my brain for someone who could help. I decided to call Judy, our Personnel Representative, who has exceptional people skills and had helped me out of some tough personnel problems in the past. I guess the tension must have been obvious in my voice, as she interrupted me, "Let me come over. I can tell this is bothering you. See you in five minutes." Just taking that first step toward solving the problem gave me a glimmer of hope.

Maybe Judy can help

How did you prepare for the meeting?

"O.K.," said Judy, "so you had a difficult discussion with Pat. Let's go back and look at the way you got ready for that meeting."

"Do you think that's really necessary? I mean I've got a problem facing me right now!"

"Maybe not," she said, "but I'd like to have the full picture, so review with me what you did."

36

"Well, last week was a busy one; when I realized that I'd scheduled a meeting with Pat for today, I just went ahead and kept our appointment."

"Let me try this one," Judy said. "You're a very conscientious manager, so tell me how you spend your time before a budget review with top management?"

"Great," I thought, "I need some specific advice about a critical personal issue, and she's going to analyze my budget review process." Just before I gave her a smart remark, I realized what she was driving at. I spent a lot of time understanding every detail, rationale, and possible alternative behind the budget my staff puts together.

"You're smiling. What's funny?" She asked.

"I am smiling, but only at what I was just thinking. It's really not funny that I spend a lot of time preparing for my budget meeting and spent very little time actually preparing for my meeting with Pat. I have been worrying about Pat, but I haven't been doing any real planning."

"I thought you'd see the point."

I could sense that Judy's insights would be of long-term value for me so I took out a pencil and pad to reserve the key ideas from our discussion for my journal. I titled it PREPARATION.

PREPARATION

DO YOUR HOMEWORK:

GATHER OBJECTIVE DATA DON'T RELY ON ASSUMPTIONS OR HEARSAY EVIDENCE.

Just as it was to Judy, my lack of preparation had been obvious to Pat. I started to squirm as I replayed a part of our conversation: "Everyone in the department has mentioned to me that you're cutting yourself off from the rest of them, and that's creating a communication barrier." I sounded like a manager--strong and informed--but when Pat had pressed me, I was forced to admit that I couldn't support what I was saying. My observations were vague, and I didn't have the facts.

Judy broke into my thoughts, "It's important to think positively as we talk and not get bogged down worrying about what has already happened. How much time can we spend on this?"

"As much time as we need. This is very important to me and I. . ."

"What's the matter?" she asked.

I couldn't believe my own ears. I was willing to spend more time talking about this with Judy than I was willing to commit to Pat. But hadn't my boss given me a book called *The One Minute Administrator?*

Judy laughed when I mentioned this. "I think you know the difference between a leader and an administrator? It's just a matter of time."

"Tell me some words that would capture what you were thinking right before the meeting with Pat." She caught me off guard so I just blurted out my immediate thoughts: "Well, I wanted to get it over with, I felt nervous and uncomfortable, I sure as heck didn't want to give in to Pat. I knew it wouldn't be any fun, and that we would end up arguing with each other."

"So when you think about it, you had a negative picture of how the meeting would go from the beginning."

She was right. I had set myself up for failure. Everything I had thought about was negative. I hadn't gone over the positive things I wanted to do and say. . . my focus had been on defensive tactics and that alone. If all I think about before a meeting is what could go wrong and how negative it will be, sure enough these things will happen.

Judy just nodded her approval. "But let's be positive."

The more I thought about it, a positive approach was exactly what my son's diving coach was spending time on--mental rehearsal and visualization. "See and feel yourself doing every detailed part of the dive

ONE MINUTE WON'T CUT IT — —
ALLOW AT LEAST 30-40 MINUTES

REHEARSE THE SESSION IN YOUR MIND— AND VISUALIZE A POSITIVE MEETING from when you walk toward the board until you hear the crowd's applause as you climb out of the pool." When I told Judy this, she asked, "Does your son ever complain about the water being too cold?"

I was ready for the next meeting; I could already feel it being successful. Judy brought me back to reality when she asked, "Roughly how many issues do you plan to bring up with Pat?"

The answer seemed obvious, "Well, all of them of course." For some reason that didn't sound right. Could Pat deal with a lot of things at once? Could I? Could Judy? It seemed so clear in retrospect. I had always advocated doing a couple of things well. Why hadn't I seen that this applied to problem-solving?

> KEEP IT SIMPLE
> ===
>
> FOCUS ON NO MORE THAN TWO ISSUES.

What were your objectives for the meeting?

I was beginning to feel comfortable about my approach to the meeting, but I still didn't have a clear picture of exactly how to talk with Pat. Judy brushed my thought aside. "Let's talk about your objective for having the coaching session with her."

"What do you mean objective? I am the manager and there is a problem that has to be solved. It's my job to solve it."

My impatience was beginning to show, but Judy persisted. "But are you there to take disciplinary action, correct an immediate problem, or what?" I hadn't thought very specifically about it, so she had me again. Seeing my discomfort, Judy said, "I've talked to a number of employees and managers about the purpose of a coaching session, and the general consensus is that its purpose is to help the employee."

MANAGERS AND EMPLOYEES AGREE THAT THE MOST IMPORTANT PURPOSE OF A COACHING SESSION IS TO DEVELOP THE EMPLOYEE

This had a more positive ring to me than some of the things I had said. If I could keep this in mind before and during any session with an employee, I knew that even sessions focused on specific performance problems would be more productive. "Great," I thought, "now can we get into what I need to do during the actual coaching session?"

But Judy sat up and started to leave. Noting the questioning look on my face she said, "I know you want more help, but I believe managers know what to do to make a coaching session successful. The problem is doing it. But if you need to bounce some ideas off of someone, I'd suggest you talk to Roy. We feel he is the best coach in the company."

"You know what to do to make a coaching session successful."

I had heard of Roy, but never actually talked to him. He was a Vice President and in a different functional area. As I dialed his number, I had a momentary feeling of embarrassment about asking for help. But his approach on the phone made me more comfortable. He said he doesn't have anything written down because each manager's approach is unique. But he talks with a lot of managers about coaching and would be glad to test my thinking out and see

Roy is the best coach in the company

if he could add anything new. I went home that night looking forward to my meeting with Roy.

TUESDAY APRIL 6

The next day Pat had returned to work, and the office was a flurry of side conversations about her trip to the doctor. Luck was with me; I had some morning meetings that kept me from having to deal with the situation. After lunch I forced myself to go to Pat and see how bad the damage was.

Setting up the 3rd. discussion with Pat

One look told me how much she was suffering. Her eyes revealed that she hadn't slept much, and her cold stare told me that she would have been more pleased to see a mortician at her desk. I cleared my throat and asked her how the doctor's appointment had gone. She immediately said, "That's personal," with a look intended to put me in my place. Small talk wasn't going to cut it so I said, "I would like to have another meeting with you to continue our discussion from the other day." Her face turned red and the muscles in her jaw tightened. I thought sure that something on her desk would come flying at me; instead she said coldly, "You're the boss."

"What a tough cookie," I thought, but I proceeded, " I want to talk about this openly, and I hope we can find a way to make things better. I really am concerned about you and your situation and feel that together we can work something out."

CHAPTER 2

MEMORIES NEVER DIE

She looked at me and, for a second, I thought she believed me. I had meant it. Then her gaze became more distant, like a curtain closing between us. I quickly interjected, "Let's both think about it for a couple of days, get our facts straight, and meet at 2:00 in my office on Thursday. Okay?" She nodded her agreement, and I felt like a small start had been made.

As I walked away from her desk, I became aware of how quiet the office was. The others on the floor were watching. Pat's problem and my response had become the center of attention, and it looked like production would continue to suffer until the issue was resolved. My meeting tomorrow with Roy couldn't come too quickly.

WEDNESDAY APRIL 7

As I got off the elevator the next day, I noticed Roy informally talking to a number of his employees. My brief observation suggested a relationship of mutual respect between these people. How much I envied that! As soon as Roy noticed me, he broke off the conversation and escorted me into his office.

Meeting with Roy

"So you want to talk about coaching?"

"Yes, and I hope you can tell me what to do because. . .".

Quietly he interrupted, "I don't plan on telling you anything. I'm hoping we can put what you already know into action. So, tell me

"I don't plan on telling you anything."

43

what you tried to accomplish with Pat during your last meeting."

"I haven't given that a lot of thought, but as nearly as I can recall, I tried to get her to see the problem and define a solution."

Smiling he said, "And she wouldn't talk about it and argued with you."

"Right! How did you know?"

"Just a lucky guess," he said. "Then what did you do?"

"I kept trying to get her to see the problem. I guess I must have sounded like a broken record, stating and restating the problem."

"Any luck?"

"Not really!"

"Don't worry about solving the problem."

"How would you react if I said you shouldn't worry about solving the problem?"

I would say that wouldn't be doing my job."

"True. But what I mean is that during the session you need to concentrate first on things other than problem-solving."

"Like what?"

Without answering me, he just asked, "Why do you feel comfortable talking to me about your problem with Pat?"

"Well, I think you understand how frustrating this is for me, and you seem to be willing to work with me in figuring this out.

44

Because I like you, I feel it's okay to discuss my problem with you."

"Whether you *like* me is not the issue."

LIKING me is not the issue

As I sat thinking about Pat, I noticed a plaque on his wall signed by a number of employees that read,

THANKS FOR BEING SUPPORTIVE

"Are you saying that I need to make a decision and provide an atmosphere of support before I can attempt to solve problems with an employee?" He just looked at me. After some silence I acknowledged, "You know that does make some sense; when I think back, there was a very supportive manager who inspired me to improve my performance." Roy then said that he tried to follow the *rule of the third*. Before this thought left me, I reached for my note pad.

RULE OF THE THIRD

DURING THE COACHING SESSION SPEND TWO-THIRDS OF YOUR TIME IN SUPPORTIVE BEHAVIORS AND ONE-THIRD OF YOUR TIME PROBLEM SOLVING

Roy continued, "There are a number of different things you can do to be viewed as supportive during a counseling session. You have to determine the best and most comfortable way for you. Your supportive actions need to be independent of the employee's support at this point in the game."

**When do I bring
up the problem?**

Feeling like I had just walked into a maze, I asked, "But when do I bring up the problem?"

I was startled by Roy's response, "Most employees are aware that a problem exists before you decide to have a conversation with them."

"Are you saying that one way of being supportive is to recognize this and give the employee credit during the conversation?"

GIVE THE
EMPLOYEE CREDIT-
90% OF EMPLOYEES
ARE AWARE A
PROBLEM
EXISTS BEFORE
YOUR COACHING
MEETING
STARTS.

"This is really helpful. Can you give me some other ideas of things I need to do to be supportive?" I asked.

"Why don't we just put our heads together and brainstorm a list of supportive behaviors?" he responded. I jotted down a heading on the pad: SUPPORTIVE BEHAVIORS.

"Where do we start?" I asked.

Roy sat forward in his chair and said, "Let's think about things which would set the tone or make the overall climate for the meeting supportive. Any ideas?"

"I can think of a few things some of my better managers did. They seemed to hold me in high positive regard and keep our discussion positive, non-threatening, and friendly in tone."

"What do you mean by positive regard?" he asked.

"They seemed to enjoy being associated with me. They liked and trusted me. In fact, one manager in particular often said things like, 'You are a good addition to the department. I enjoy working with you."

"Wow, I would feel supported if I worked for a manager like that," he said. "Why don't you add that to your list?"

SUPPORTIVE
BEHAVIORS

TALK ABOUT
POSITIVE
    REGARDS --
EXPRESS
ACCEPTANCE OF
THE EMPLOYEE-
THE VALUE YOU
PLACE ON THE
ASSOCIATION

"Now, how about the non-threatening tone you mentioned?"

"Yes," I said, "this particular manager was able to keep our discussions positive in tone-- even when they were very difficult or involved a difference of opinion. He'd say things like; 'My concern is not to place blame but to solve the problem. I want to make this a constructive conversation and focus on attacking the problem, not each other."

KEEP THE EXCHAGE POSITIVE: STATE ISSUES IN A GENTLE, NON-AGGRESSIVE, NON-THREATENING WAY, BE PATIENT !!

"It wasn't just what he said with words. You knew he meant it because he worked so hard during the discussion to make it happen."

"That's super," he said, "That's my intent, but sometimes it seems hard to clearly and believably communicate it to an employee. But, that's what makes this business fun. Let me add one to your list. To me support is being flexible and making the problem-solving process a joint one between two people and not just a one-way street."

BE COLLABORATIVE/ FLEXIBLE: MAINTAIN TEAM-WORK, MUTUAL PROBLEM-SOLVING AND A "LET'S SOLVE THIS TOGETHER" ATTITUDE

"Let me piggyback on that and add the word collaborative. The employee and I need to strive for a 'let's solve this together' attitude."

"I like that," he affirmed.

"Let's get something to drink and keep going," I said. "This is exciting. You really have some good ideas."

As we sat there a thought occurred to me and I said, "Roy, I would like to get more specific about what actually happens during the session."

"I agree. What are some of your ideas?"

"I often think about how much time I talk and how much time I allow the employee to talk during our meetings."

"That's interesting," Roy said, "I expect the employee to carry 40% of the conversation load. So the 40-60 rule is what I try to live by."

THE 40-60 RULE

SHARE THE CONVERSATION LOAD:

MANAGERS SHOULD TALK NO MORE THAN 60% OF THE TIME.

"I noticed that you asked me a lot of questions when we started to talk. It got me thinking and gave me the feeling that you were interested."

"Right," he said.

"O.K., we're on a roll. What's next?"

"How about simply helping the employee?" Roy asked.

"I don't understand."

"If you can become a resource to the employee, either by providing assistance, being accessible, or being willing to try something new, would this mean anything?"

"You bet," I said, "this would feel better to me than being left alone to resolve the issue."

> BECOME A RESOURCE TO THE EMPLOYEE: PROVIDE HELP, BE AVAILABLE, AND BE WILLING TO TRY A NEW WAY

Then another thought occurred to me, "Don't you also have to be optimistic and believe in the employee's potential?" I asked.

"Absolutely! If you don't communicate confidence and encouragement to the employee, who will?"

> COMMUNICATE ENCOURAGEMENT AND CONFIDENCE IN THE EMPLOYEE'S POTENTIAL

"Roy, what bothers me is that I may sound phoney or plastic, but I think what helps make this all legitimate is a genuine concern for the employee's interests and objectives. If I am careful to try and protect the employees rights, help them achieve their objectives, and receive fair consideration, then I shouldn't have to worry about being viewed as phoney."

CHAPTER 2

MEMORIES NEVER DIE

Roy just smiled, "I couldn't have put it any better."

"Roy, you know, every once in a while I think about Pat. She really has had a tough break in her life, and she must feel very upset and used. That's got to be a heavy burden."

Roy smiled, "I don't think you can be supportive without doing what you have just done--walk in the other person's shoes."

"You simply need to treat the employees' feelings and concerns with dignity and give them fair consideration," Roy said.

"Another thing I thought of while you were talking is helping employees maintain positive self-esteem. That's a little different from the things you have already listed, but just as important. How do you see that playing out?" asked Roy.

"I think you would have to express appreciation for employees--their knowledge, skills, and abilities. A piece of this would be acknowledging the employee's contribution and role in the work unit."

LET EMPLOYEES KNOW YOU ARE AWARE OF AND SENSITIVE TO THEIR INTERESTS, NEEDS, OBJECTIVES, AND ASPIRATIONS

EMPATHIZE WITH THE EMPLOYEE'S FEELINGS AND EMOTIONS ABOUT THE ISSUE OR CONCERN

MAINTAIN THE EMPLOYEES' POSITIVE SELF-ESTEEM: TELL THEM THEY ARE IMPORTANT AND THAT YOU VALUE THEM

THE COACH

LISTEN:
UNDERSTAND
WHAT EMPLOYEES
ARE SAYING
AND GIVE
THEM FULL
CONSIDERATION
AND
ATTENTION

OWN UP:
SHARE THE
RESPONSIBILITY
FOR THE
CURRENT STATE
OF AFFAIRS
WHEN
APPROPRIATE

"You don't have to do all these things!"

"And how could I have forgotten this one? Listening to the employee is the highest compliment."

Roy responded, "Listening is really a big part of the 40-60 rule we talked about earlier."

I was starting to run out of ideas when Roy leaned forward with an excited expression and said, "How about 'owning up'?"

Puzzled, I said, "Like in a bet?"

"No, like in sharing responsibility for the current state of affairs," Roy responded.

I slid back in my chair to a more comfortable position and yawned, "I am drained of ideas."

"So am I," he said, "but I think you have developed an excellent list for yourself, and I know you can do it. Just remember that you don't have to do all of these things we have talked about in one session and that you do have to be yourself and not use a script."

"Roy, you've been a great help. Would you like a copy of the list?" He smiled and said, "Sure. I can add it to the others."

"Others? Are there others?"

52

"Yes, and I must admit that there is not a significant difference among all the lists I have received copies of over the years. But don't look so defeated. You have created an original for you."

"Why are the lists so similar?" I asked.

"Because coaching is really no mystery; you have to trust yourself to do what you already know."

"You have to rely on your own list as you put these things into practice during the live session. My hunch is that you can and will do it. I wish you luck."

I felt mentally exhausted, but elated. The greatest coach in our company had just helped me understand how I could reach out and connect with Pat. I knew it wouldn't be easy, but I was excited about the opportunities and challenges that my next meeting with Pat would present.

> MANAGERS KNOW WHAT TO DO DURING A SUCCESSFUL COACHING SESSION — THE PROBLEM IS ALLOWING YOURSELF TO DO IT

THURSDAY APRIL 8

**3rd. discussion
with Pat**

Thursday morning was dismal. The rain lashed at my office windows and the sky was a forbidding grey. As Pat entered my office, her cold stare added to the chill. The tension mounted, and I could feel all the confidence and good ideas I had been developing over the past few days fade as quickly as sun behind the clouds. Concerned that the meeting could easily get out of control, I gave myself a quick, silent pep talk. "Get a hold of yourself. Relax. You know what needs to be done, so let's get on with it." I cleared my throat and said, "Pat, I don't imagine you are finding this any more comfortable than I am." Silence, my God, is she going to stare at the floor the whole meeting? Well, there is nothing to do but plod onward. "Let me start. I know things have been tough for you, and I want to help."

"leave me alone"

"You can help by leaving me alone and telling the rest of your gossipmongers to do likewise," she blurted out.

**I can't accept
that**

"I understand you want to be left alone when things are difficult, but you need to know that I can't accept that. The kind of help I can offer you is understanding. You got a raw deal, but now we need to figure out where we can go from here."

"What do you know about raw deals? Your life looks pretty comfortable to me."

"Pat, maybe I don't know a lot about raw deals firsthand, but I believe that I can help you move beyond this experience. Something different needs to be done now, and we need to work out what that is."

54

CHAPTER 2

MEMORIES NEVER DIE

Wow!! The intensity in her look reminded me of a cornered jackal poised for the attack. I knew we were at a critical point--what to say--"Trust yourself," I heard a voice inside me, leading me on. "Pat, if you continue to view me as the enemy rather than as a partner, we're not going to get anywhere."

"Enemy or partner?"

"Well, you're sure not a friend," she shot back.

"Perhaps you don't feel that we can team up again. That's your choice. But I am willing to respect you as a professional employee and to treat you fairly--and that's all I'm asking from you."

The silence was fraught with emotion. A base drum had replaced the clock on my wall. I could hardly hear Pat as she said, "That's all I've every asked for--to be treated like everyone else. I may have made mistakes, but I'll be damned if I'll give others the satisfaction of gloating over them. To hell with them, all of them! I got myself into this, and I'll get myself out--with no help from you or from them, thank you very much."

"If I didn't really want to help you Pat, it would be awfully easy for me to say, 'Fine, I am glad you're willing to take care of things, and have a nice day.' I am not going to do that because I feel responsible for some of the things that have happened to you, and I want to play a part in figuring out how we can turn things in this department around."

"I feel responsible"

"Just tell your spies to lay off. If they would quit being so nosey and stop acting like a

55

bunch of old women, things would work themselves out."

"So, Pat, you're saying that it's all their fault?"

"Well, what about Rico? Why just this morning he. . ."

"Wait, Pat," I interrupted, "before we talk about Rico. I want you to hear that I am willing to help, but you have to do some things differently here at work, not just depend on Rico and the others to change."

"What if I don't want to do things differently, what if I don't want to work here, what if I want my old job back?" she blurted out with intensity that I had never seen before.

I paused a second and then asked, "Is your old job available?" Her silence answered the question. "As far as your working here, I believe you can play an important part in our group. I want to be as clear and honest as I can about that point."

"I've got to work, I want to work, I can't afford to start all over again, but I still have my pride left and I'll be damned if I will give anyone the satisfaction of seeing me crawl. You'll have to fire me first."

"I don't expect you to crawl, and I certainly don't want to fire you. I just want you to do your job in a professional way, using the skills you have with people the way I've seen you work in the past. You helped me out of some rough spots, and now I want to do the same for you. But you do have co-workers, and your job requires close cooperation with them."

"You have to change"

"What if I don't want to do things differently?"

CHAPTER 2

MEMORIES NEVER DIE

"I know I have shut them out," she sighed. "I guess I was just trying to hurt them--the way they had hurt me. Not one of them helped me when I needed it, especially Rico."

"Okay, let's really look at this. Just exactly who have you been hurting?"

"Let's really look at this"

"I hope all of them," she said with a glare.

"Why? What have they said to you?"

"They haven't said anything."

"Well, it must really be getting to them then. Let me ask the question again."

Pat's shallow laugh echoed off my walls. "Isn't that ironic? Here I try to get them and wind up hurting myself--what a joke!"

Minutes ticked by, but self-discovery had been key in my growth as an employee, and I wanted the same opportunity for Pat. I wasn't ready for her next outburst.

"How do you expect me to work with these people? Can't you transfer me back where I was?"

"That's not an alternative, Pat. I think you know that. We need to figure out how to make the best out of your present job." Retreating once more, Pat's gaze returned to the floor. She mumbled a few words that were hard to make out. . . I don't think she wanted me to hear it. I said, "Look, Pat, let's not defeat ourselves before we try. Why don't you tell me why the work in the department is not getting done on time?"

"You tell me why"

57

She didn't answer right away, but this time I waited, giving her a chance to sort through some of the thoughts and feelings that seemed to be churning inside her. When she spoke again, it was more softly, "That's pretty tough. I mean, isn't it like signing my own death warrant?"

"Pat, if I wanted to fire you I could. I just think that you're smart enough to help me get to the bottom of this."

"I suppose you're right."

Her words came more easily now. "I suppose you're right," she said, "but if it's not hurting anyone but me, I'm sort of defeating my own purpose."

"It's also hurting our team's productivity, but not as much as it's giving you a negative image in the company."

At that, she snapped back, "How much worse can it be?"

"Believe me, I think people have pretty much seen through Bob and aren't dwelling on the past nearly as much as you think. From now on, I would worry about the effect your actions are having on your future."

Pat just smiled and said, "So it appears my withdrawal from the team has slowed up the whole chain of production."

I calmly replied, "You hit the nail right on the head."

"O.K., I can handle the others, but working with Rico. . . he's a real. . . well I won't say it. . . I just won't say what I think about him."

58

"That's where we need to focus our attention. How you get along with your peers is ultimately going to affect what people think of you and whether they cooperate with you. Is there anything that you could do differently?"

"Why don't you talk to him?" Pat pleaded.

I could feel the burden being shifted back to me, but I persisted. "Perhaps we shouldn't rule that out. For now I want to go back to my original question, "Is there anything *you* can do?"

"What can you do?"

"O.K.," Pat said, "*I 'll* talk to him. Isn't that good enough? I thought that's what you wanted. Why are you looking at me so funny?"

"Because I would like to know more specifically when and how you plan to do this."

"When and how?"

After another long silence Pat responded, "I think I'll ask Rico to have lunch and tell him that I want to try and work more closely with him in the future. The only thing I can do then is to see how he responds and whether we can come up with some different things to do. Is that acceptable?"

"For now," I said, "that is a really good start. Do you think you can schedule this sometime this week?"

"That's a good start."

"So you don't trust me?"

"No, that's not it. I want you to know that I do trust you, but it's important for me to know when I can expect some progress."

"I'll try to get together with Rico in the next two days," she said.

"I think that would be a good start. This won't only help you, Pat, but it will be an important step in helping the entire team be more effective. I know you'll give it your best shot. Why don't we meet after you have lunch with Rico and talk about what happened and how I can help?"

There was a lengthy pause. . ."O.K., I appreciate what you are trying to do."

End of the meeting

As Pat walked out of the office, I felt a tremendous sense of relief. Our meeting had gone well--not perfectly, but we had made a start. It had taken just short of one hour, but hadn't seemed as long as our last meeting. Luckily, I didn't have anything else scheduled this time to add extra pressure.

I decided to get a drink of water and then unwind while I reflected on our meeting and captured the key points in my journal. As I turned the corner, Rico about ran into me. "Hey," he said, "heard you were having a meeting with Pat--sure hope you smoothed things out. It has been a real bummer working with her."

Rico's smile was more cynical than friendly. I wasn't ready for another long discussion, so I brushed him off with, "She'll probably want to talk to you about how the two of you can best work together. I would suggest you take seriously what she has to say."

60

CHAPTER 2

MEMORIES NEVER DIE

"Great," he said snidely, "I've been waiting for my chance to work closer with her."

I just ignored the cheap innuendo. "Just give her a fair shot at talking to you, O.K.?"

"Sure, count on me."

Rico's attitude helped me sense what Pat was confronting constantly, and it was upsetting to say the least. I put my feelings aside temporarily, so that I could focus on capturing some thoughts in my journal while the discussion with Pat was still fresh on my mind. As I took the journal out of my briefcase, I immediately began to feel better. Where to start. Pat's conversation was sincere. I began a new page and titled it: "Problem Solving."

O.K., so the tone of the conversation had allowed us to look at the problems in a constructive fashion, but there had to be more to it than that. Roy said I would know what to do. . .but what did I do? As I thought back on the conversation, I felt one of the key priorities had been keeping the conversation channels open between Pat and me.

PROBLEM SOLVING

EXPRESSING SUPPORT ALLOWS THE EMPLOYEE TO PERCEIVE YOU AS GENUINELY INTERESTED AND FACILITATES A MORE HONEST DISCUSSION OF THE PROBLEM

KEEP A HIGH LEVEL OF SUPPORT AND INVOLVEMENT THROUGHOUT THE CONVERSATION

KEEP THE FOCUS ON THE PROBLEM

Pat and I both talked openly about some pretty touchy subjects. But Pat kept raising matters which I felt were irrelevant to the issue at hand and sometimes didn't seem to understand the exact nature of the problem. I remembered thinking at the time that I had to help us keep focused on the problem, even though Pat wanted to take the conversation in different directions.

CLARIFY EXPECTATIONS AND NEEDS

It seemed to help when I stated my expectations in this situation. Pat seemed to really take note of these.

But beyond that, how could I have forgotten that look in Pat's eye when I told her I wanted her to help me analyze the problem. She seemed pleased that we both had something to contribute to a better understanding of the situation.

ACKNOWLEDGE THE EMPLOYEE'S AWARENESS OF THE PROBLEM

Now that I think back on it, this approach did seem to keep us focused and created a team approach to the problem. I guess if I hadn't

CHAPTER 2

MEMORIES NEVER DIE

done this, she might have felt put down, like she wasn't too smart; that would have been extremely difficult. The only other thing that kept us focused was my wanting us both to understand as much about the problem as we could. I was afraid that too many rumors, assumptions, and opinions were floating around, so I wanted us to agree on just exactly what the facts were. I could remember a math professor once saying, "A problem well defined is a problem half solved."

DEFINE THE TOPIC AND ISSUES

With both of us thinking and discussing the specifics behind the problem, we couldn't help but keep focused.

Even though we had defined the problem, Pat still didn't think it was such a big deal. Now I remember it wasn't until we discussed the impact the problem was having on her image and the department that she started to take it seriously. Looking at the impact seemed to be a critical turning point in the conversation.

ESTABLISH THE IMPACT

It made the whole issue more personal and important. What was it my psychology professor used to say? Internalize. Yes, she had started to own the problem. She did a personal value analysis. I felt really excited about this discovery. I sat back for a few minutes and considered this point. If we hadn't discussed the impact, I bet she would have continued to consider the problem mine, instead of hers or ours.

The conversation seemed to get a little easier from that point on. The next things we did were to try and determine some specific things that could be done differently. Pretty straight forward, I thought, but the key was we didn't stop until we both felt like we had a good plan developed.

INITIATE
ACTION
PLANS

At the time, I remember thinking, "Is she really going to give this a good try, or is she just leading me on?" So I asked her if she was going to try it. Sounds pretty simple, but I wonder how many times in the past I had assumed that an employee would do something--unfortunately too many.

GET
A
COMMITMENT

As I think about it now, there were plenty of times when I wanted to get really negative and let Pat know what would happen if she didn't shape up--why didn't I? That's interesting. I guess I never reacted too favorably to what I used to call "doom messages," so I didn't say anything to Pat. Wait a minute, yes I did. I tried to keep it positive and let her know what good would result if she was successful in trying our plan. That didn't seem to hurt; in fact, she seemed to appreciate having some additional reasons for trying to follow through on the plans. I can imagine how she would have reacted if I'd reverted to a more harsh and primitive approach to managing the situation.

My hand hit the glass of water as I put the pencil down, but I caught it before it tipped. I continued to mentally replay the meeting. There were times during the conversation that Pat tried to pass the buck and blame others or her situation for the problem. Every time this happened, it was like a warning flag being waved in front of my face. I knew that if she was permitted to deny responsibility for her actions, she would never own any responsibility for the problem. She also tried to give me some reasons why nothing could be done about the current situation. This to me was the same; it kept us from coming up with a solution. I came to realize that excuses and obstacles could have kept us both from coming to grips with the problem and from figuring out a way to deal with it. My approach was to listen to the excuse or obstacle she presented and then redirect the conversation to an area we could control-- namely, how she behaved.

EMPHASIZE
POSITIVE
CONSEQUENCES

CONFRONT
EXCUSES
AND
RESISTANCE

Thinking hard, I could only remember how I tried to end the conversation, wanting to continue to work with her towards improvement and setting up a specific time for review.

DON'T GIVE UP — FOLLOW UP!!

FRIDAY APRIL 9

Lunch with Rico

Wow! It was a mental struggle to get all that down on paper. It was more tiring than the actual conversation, but I knew my list would be helpful in future conversations with Pat, as well as with other employees. I ended the day with the sense that I had done all that I could. The next step was up to Pat.

When Pat bounded into my office the next afternoon, I couldn't believe the difference. She had a grin from ear to ear and a sparkle in her eye that I had forgotten she possessed.

"Just wanted to update you on my lunch meeting with Rico. It was a little difficult at first. I could tell he didn't trust me, so I told him that was okay. I'd *prove* to him that I could do the job. We talked about ways we could work together, and by the end of lunch he asked me whether we should continue our discussion over dinner!"

"That's great, Pat! Now you're sounding like the coach. I'm really glad you met with Rico, but you will be cautious about the type of relationship you build won't you? I'd hate to see Rico turn into another Bob." I

CHAPTER 2

MEMORIES NEVER DIE

grimaced as I recalled Rico's self-centered remarks about Pat. "Perhaps I'd better talk to him."

Pat interrupted my musing with a genuine sense of concern. "I know how this must look to you--but there are still two sides to this story. I know how difficult it is to mix business with pleasure. If Rico has something other than business in mind, I'll be very clear about what I want. A work relationship that helps both of us do our jobs is what I'm interested in. I appreciate your concern, but I think I'll be okay."

"There are two sides to this story."

I found it hard to believe this was the same Pat who had caused me so much anxiety. I'd felt our discussion had gone well, but this was a miracle! Maybe, she would be all right. "Thanks for sharing that with me, Pat. I feel more confident now than I ever have before that you're going to be a wonderful asset to the department! Welcome back!"

Pat just smiled. "Thanks for listening. I think I'd better get back to work. I have a lot of catching up to do."

"Thanks for listening"

It all seemed too good to be true, so I kept my eyes on Pat and Rico--and the rest of the department. The atmosphere didn't seem quite real--I'm sure everyone was waiting for some new crisis--but it did seem as if some new efforts at teamwork were being made. And Pat and Rico seemed to be working well together, so my heart dropped when Rico asked if he could speak to me privately. I'd been feeling so good. I really wasn't ready to deal with a new problem.

THE COACH

"What is it, Rico? Is there a problem between you and Pat?"

"No. Not at all. I've just been feeling really bad about what I said to you about her. She's not at all what I thought, and her work is doing a lot for this department. I just wanted you to know. . .".

Rico disappeared as quickly as he had come, perhaps a bit embarrassed that he'd let his macho exterior slip for a bit. I just shook my head. Who would have predicted it?

A twist of fate

But the drama and irony of this whole situation wasn't quite over. At dinner that evening I proudly described to my family how excited I was about my new-found leadership success. I must admit I was beginning to feel like I was getting my department back under control. As the evening wore on, I was mentally reviewing my plans for a meeting the next day with the entire department. Just as I began to envision my opening statement, my spouse, who loves to watch the local evening news, yelled at me "Hey, come and see this." As I entered the TV room and looked at the screen, I was shocked. Why sure enough, it was Bob, our old Marketing Director, being interviewed by a reporter. "What is he doing on TV?" I thought to myself. "I thought he had left town." I turned up the volume and listened intently to the interview. The camera angle changed, and I noticed that two members from our board of directors were also talking to the reporter. "What the heck was going on?" I sat glued to the TV. Everyone in the room was asking me "What are they saying. . what are they saying?" It seemed like the

Bob on T.V

68

interview was about a buyout or merger of our company by some new investors. . . and then the interview was over in a flash. "Merger mania" in the business world has hit the medium-size companies as well as the big Fortune 500, I thought. I guess Bob is as well connected in the business world as he said. He must have moved fast after he was fired in order to retaliate and to be able to gather enough investors and force the board members into a sale. From what I heard of the interview, the stockholders will certainly make money on this deal. . . but it will be pure chaos having Bob as our CEO. . . why he is a marketing man, not a corporate executive, or so it had seemed. The shock of these swift business maneuverings was too much for me to fathom. I retired for the evening, anxious to get to work the next day to catch the fallout.

A merger!!

Bob as C.E.O.

I didn't sleep a whole lot that night. My mind was reeling about the thoughts of the new leadership in our company. When I rushed into the office the next morning, I was anxious to get my group together for the meeting we had planned. I noticed the main floor was alive with activity. Everyone had crowded up to a bulletin board in the main hall that was full of announcements. I planned to go down later and read through them myself, when the crowd thinned out a little. I probably wouldn't have sensed anything out of the ordinary but the elevator became strangely quiet as I got on, and I felt suddenly uncomfortable; for a minute I thought maybe I had forgotten to comb my hair. When I got to my office, Pat was there waiting for me. Not knowing what else to

No sleep tonight

do, I asked her to come in and sit down. She looked tired and unsettled. I groaned inwardly, wondering what new crisis was upon us. I waited expectantly and finally Pat began.

"You haven't heard then?"

"No, I guess I haven't, though people did seem to be acting a bit strangely on the elevator," I said.

**Woops!!
Pat is the new
Director**

"Well you better sit down then; this may come as a bit of a shocker." I did as Pat suggested, and then she showed me Bob's re-organization announcement for our group. It had Bob's signature on it. I am sure my face went as white as the paper I was reading. "Oh crap," I heard myself saying. Bob was making Pat the director for my department along with two other departments. I was stunned and flabbergasted. Thoughts raced through my mind about how I had been treating Pat during the last few weeks. At first I thought the worst. . . . "My career is down the tubes . . . maybe I can update my resume."

I guess the panic on my face provoked Pat to speak. "Are you all right?"

"Oh, sure, sure, a . . . a . . . congratulations. . . . I mean this must be exciting for you". . . I couldn't think of anything else to say to her.

Pat said, "Thanks. . . . there is something I would like to explain to you. I know this looks like things have happened pretty fast, but you should know that Bob's plans to take over this company were in the works even before he was hired. He told two or three people about his ideas right before he left and swore us to secrecy until he was in the driver's seat with the investors and had the financing together. Bob believed that the CEO was too cautious and traditional and was really holding down the growth potential of the company. I guess they finally had a big argument and blowout. . . . That's why Bob left."

"Holy smokes," I interrupted, "how did you know about all this?"

"Well, Bob seemed to feel that my abilities and drive fit in well with his plans. . . . I guess the chemistry was right."

I couldn't keep up with what Pat was saying. The implications of this change began to settle in. When Pat finished talking, she asked me, "How are you doing? You've been pretty quiet."

I took a deep breath. "How will I explain this to my department?"

"What do you mean?"

"I think they will wonder if I am going to keep my job now that you are the boss."

What about me?

Pat was quiet for a minute before she responded, "I want you to know that I need you right where you are. You have taught me a lot about leadership."

"But won't a lot of people be wondering if you will try to get even for the way you've been treated?"

"Well, it has been tough, but I think we need to pick up the pieces and go on together. As the leader of this department, you have my full support."

All I could think about was how close I had come to throwing in the towel with Pat. Now the roles were reversed. I felt more vulnerable. . . and, at the same time felt a deep appreciation for the meaning of support and partnership.

Pat's voice broke into my thoughts. "I believe that you had a department meeting scheduled for this morning." I nodded hesitantly. "Let's talk to people together. It's going to be important for us to work as a team, and this will be a good place to start."

"O.K., see you at 10:30."

This could be interesting

Pat's departure left me with my thoughts. "What a way to go into a weekend...what the heck, I did my best with Pat. No need to look back, this could be interesting."

CHAPTER 3

THE 8 - STEP MODEL

Although the story you have just read is fictional, the coaching process is not. It is based on over eight years of working with leaders in our consulting and training programs and on an extensive organizational research effort. Specifically, our staff has observed and surveyed 3,000 managers and more than 7,000 employees on this subject. In addition, an in-depth study was completed in 1986 that compared the behaviors of highly effective coaches and their employees to those of less effective coaches and their employees.[1] The data from this study produced 47 categories of leader behavior that play a role in the success of a coaching session. This information has been condensed for the practicing leader. Many of the main conclusions were presented in the preceding fictional account, and the remainder of the book is based on information collected from observations, surveys, and research analysis.

We will begin then with an 8-step coaching model that represents much of what we have learned about the coaching process. See Illustration 3.1. These 8 steps serve as a communication road map. In subsequent sections, supporting coaching concepts will clarify other key leadership behaviors needed to make the 8-step communication model successful.

[1]For a comprehensive presentation of the methodology, the results, and a current literature review, see Stowell, S. J. Leadership and the Coaching Process in Organizations. A dissertation submitted to the Department of Psychology, University of Utah. December, 1986.

Illustration   3.1

EIGHT STEP

COACHING MODEL

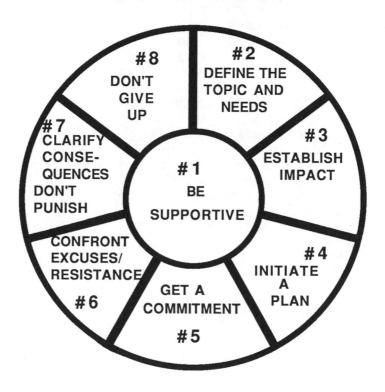

CHAPTER 3

THE 8 - STEP MODEL

STEP ONE:

BE SUPPORTIVE

Simply put, supportiveness *is not* an option when it comes to coaching. The success of a coaching discussion with an employee about needed changes or additions to performance is determined by the employee's perception of the leader's supportiveness. No other factor is as important as this. The highly effective leaders that we studied devoted *half* of their time and attention to expressing some sort of supportive message. They were basically able to do two things: (1) express this apparently unconditional positive support very clearly to the employee, and (2) initiate a strong and clear problem-solving discussion without being punitive or demeaning to the employee.

"Support is a decision, not an emotional exchange"

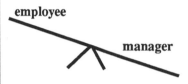

In all likelihood, this step is not a surprise to most people. Many coaching models include this step in one way or another. However, the fact that it is such a significant and dominant step is a key discovery. Support and the strong emphasis that we give it constitute the most distinguishing feature of our coaching process. This step has been placed at the center of our model. It symbolically touches all of the other steps because highly effective leaders express support as they move through the problem-solving process (represented by the "outer" ring of steps). Any one coaching session can contribute to the employee's overall perception of the leader's willingness to be supportive. Supportiveness needs to precede the discussion and can be obviously acted out once the coaching is over. Our evidence demonstrates that supportiveness is a long-term effort.

The level of support employees attribute to managers is a matter of degrees. Employees always have a feeling about the supportiveness of their managers. The success of discussions with employees about needed changes or additions to their performance is determined by the employees' perception of the managers' supportiveness. No other factor is as important. Because we have no option--this perception cannot be avoided--the wise manager seeks to engage in behaviors that result in being viewed as supportive. To improve your effectiveness as a coach, improve on the level of support as perceived by the employee.

But how do you show that you are supportive? You have a number of choices. The effective managers we studied engaged in ten distinct caring behaviors. These managers paid attention to the quality of the relationship and did things to maintain a healthy exchange. The ten supportive behaviors are listed and described.

10 SUPPORTIVE BEHAVIORS

Collaboration/ Flexibility

COLLABORATION/FLEXIBILITY:
Responsibility is mutually shared for assignments, tasks, and changes, with a willingness to compromise and work together.

Helping/ Assisting

HELPING/ASSISTING:
The leader is willing to help out, provide resources, and be available for future consultation.

76

EMPATHY/UNDERSTANDING:
The leader treats the employee's feelings, concerns, obstacles, and difficulties with dignity.

Empathy/
Understanding

RECOGNITION OF EMPLOYEE'S VALUE:
The leader expresses appreciation, believes the employee is an important part of the team, and gives the employee a positive sense of self-esteem.

Recognition of
Employee's
Value

LISTENING/INTERACTION:
Willing to give the employee full attention, the leader asks lots of questions and gives the employee time to express ideas, reactions, and suggestions.

Listening/
Interaction

RECOGNITION OF EMPLOYEE'S INTERESTS/GOALS:
The leader is aware of the employee's interests, individual needs, objectives, and aspirations.

Recognition of
Employee's
Interests/Goals

POSITIVE FEEDBACK/CREDIT:
The leader is willing to point out successes and give the employee credit for specific past achievements.

Positive Feedback/
Credit

Encouragement/
Optimism

Postive
Exchange

Owning some
Responsibility/
Openness

ENCOURAGEMENT/OPTIMISM:
The leader is hopeful, reassuring, and believes that the situation can be solved as a result of the employee's effort.

POSITIVE EXCHANGE:
The leader's friendly approach focuses on issues in a gentle, non-aggressive, non-threatening, non-judgmental way.

OWNING SOME RESPONSIBILITY/OPENNESS:
The leader accepts responsibility for contributing to the situation and doesn't blame it all on the employee. They share important information and insight, and the leader shows trust.

In Illustration 3.2, these ten supportive behaviors are arranged in a hierarchy of importance. Although not a strict ordering, the most important behavior is collaboration/flexibility.

In our studies we have found that when a leader neglects these behaviors or does the opposite by harsh, aggressive, and non-supportive comments and actions, the employee develops a perception that the leader is not a partner and, in fact, is non-supportive or even adversarial. One other detail we have noticed is that effective coaching experiences correlated highly with the leader and employee having a history of working well together and viewing each other in a positive light.

Illustration 3.2

THE HIERARCHY OF
SUPPORTIVE LEADER BEHAVIORS

1. COLLABORATION/
   FLEXIBILITY

2. HELPING/
   ASSISTING

3. EMPATHY/
   UNDERSTANDING

4. RECOGNITION OF
   EMPLOYEE VALUE

5. LISTENING/INTERACTION

6. RECOGNITION OF EMPLOYEE'S
   INTERESTS/GOALS

7. POSITIVE FEEDBACK/CREDIT

8. ENCOURAGEMENT/OPTIMISM

9. POSITIVE EXCHANGE

10. OWNING SOME RESPONSIBILITY/OPENNESS

THE COACH

Hey, I'm not caring!

Some people may look at this and say, "Hey, I am just not a caring and supportive type of person." This creates a special challenge to be more conscious and deliberate in expressing some support during and after a coaching session. Other people may look at this step, dismiss it, and say in a sarcastic tone, "I get loved at home." No matter how much people choose to deny it, a little support at work, especially from the boss, feels incredibly good and certainly contributes to one's self-confidence and esteem. These are important elements when things are not going well or when the leader wants to bring about change. It may be that higher level managers feel more cared for and valued by the organization than middle and lower level members of the organization (because of their status, perks, and creature comforts), but don't be deceived by these physical trappings of support. Recognize that expressions of support will be interpreted as helpful at all levels in the organization.

Just to be clear, we are not saying that people in your organization have to "like you." We are not talking about the leader receiving support and caring behaviors; we are talking about the leader's willingness and courage to give support even in the face of adversity, disappointment, and problems. This is what makes leadership a challenge--to move off and beyond the concern or problem and to enlist the support and cooperation of others as effectively and rapidly as possible. Even though you may have feelings of frustration or even anger, you will need to let them go in

80

CHAPTER 3

THE 8 - STEP MODEL

order to enlist the genuine willingness and commitment of your employees to make your unit better. If you feel the employee pulling back or withdrawing, you will need to be persistent in clarifying your supportive intentions. You may even want to make your intentions and the employee's resistance a focal point of the conversation for a time in order to build a supportive base.

STEP TWO:

DISCUSS THE ISSUES AND EXPECTATIONS

Feedback almost always feels personal: "You know you're ugly and your Mom dresses you funny."

TIPS:

Don't accuse

Allow employees "air time"

Be specific, descriptive, non-hostile

Step 2 is the first substantive problem-solving step. The purpose of Step 2 is to create a mutually understood picture of what's happening. When giving feedback and discussing the concern or developmental opportunity with the employee, a few tips may be helpful:

1. Don't start with an accusation that will create a head-on collision, instant defensiveness, and an argument. ("You were really lousy at handling questions in that meeting.") Begin with a more natural introduction. ("I want to talk about the way you handle questions in meetings.")

2. Give the employee some "air time," time to react, vent, or defend. All the employee wants you to do is acknowledge that "it isn't easy being an employee" and that "it's a real jungle out there." If the employee does seem a bit defensive say, "I can tell that you have had some difficulties, challenges, obstacles, etc." This will be seen as supportive.

3. State your concern or issue in a specific, descriptive, non-hostile way. Focus on relevant here-and-now topics. Offer your observations and data. Take ownership for it. A vital issue, and one that a lot of well-meaning leaders miss, is that you need to be prepared to accept some responsibility for the current situation as well. Acknowledge that it is very possible that your own actions or omissions may have helped create part of the problem. A lot of leaders play a game, "It isn't my fault. . . Don't blame me. . ." Work

and jobs are complex these days, and it would be very foolish to blame it *all* on the employee.

4. Use the time in Step 2 to gather additional data from the employee. Build your understanding of the situation with any specific information or insight that the employee can provide. Be on the lookout for preliminary excuses and justifications. Excuses are normal and natural when anyone questions or doubts the effectiveness of our behavior. They indicate that the employee is beginning to deal with some uncomfortable or harsh realities. We all want to avoid this anguish, and so we try to avoid the issue or offer excuses for our behavior. . . it's perfectly normal. The leader needs to support this with some understanding and then move on to the rest of the steps.

Gather employee input

5. Simply restate your information and interpretation of the issue you want to discuss. If you have planned well, you will have gathered some reliable firsthand data that will be believable to the employee and will make all other data sound like "hearsay" evidence. Remember, too, that this discussion is another step in the information-gathering process. If you don't treat the employee's information with dignity and respect, the employee *will* believe that your judgment is set in concrete. If the employee has information that you can trust, then respond authentically. Remember that *a problem well defined is half solved.*

Restate your information

**Clarify
expectations**

6. Next it is very important that you state or restate your expectations, what it is that you "want." The hard/measurable side sounds like a business mission or goal statement, and the softer side includes a statement of your values and the positive thing that you are trying to create in your department. This represents the unique contribution you and your group can make to the company. This is a future-oriented statement that could include functional values (quality, customer relations, accuracy, or creativity), or it could include personal values and wishes (growth, satisfaction, recognition, skill building, or risk taking). The point is to let others around you know what you are working toward and what is important to you in both the short and long run. An example might be, "I expect everyone in our unit to act like a *team* player and share information as quickly as possible.

The objective of this step is to achieve mutual understanding and to allow both leader and employee perceptions to be expressed. Leaders should try to make this a non-evaluative and descriptive review of the opportunities or concerns. This step should focus on relevant here-and-now issues and not deal with historical performance issues (the leader is making an error by delaying a discussion of events in the distant past). It is critical that leaders be specific, assertive, and fair to themselves as well as the employee. The manager can really prepare the employee for change by beginning with good information and gathering additional data from the employee.

Some leaders love this step and find it very easy. Unfortunately, some even take delight in criticizing the performance of others. Other managers find this step extremely difficult and awkward because its confrontive nature can create some anxiety and controversy. The suggestions offered here provide leaders who are either overly aggressive or timid an alternative for presenting the issue and giving feedback.

It is unmistakably clear that leaders should deal with essentially one issue at a time in the coaching session and not commit the "overload" error that is discussed in another unit. The leader can achieve greater success by breaking monumental issues apart and generating some momentum on a manageable piece. We also believe that, at this early stage in the coaching sequence, it *is not* important for the employee to be in total agreement with your perceptions. Don't push too hard and expect the employee to give in. After all, it is the employee's effort and actions that are being examined here, and he/she needs a little space to assimilate your points.

Concentrate on one issue

Finally, the key things you can do to communicate adequate supportiveness during this step are to listen; clarify your intentions (that you are not here to rake the employee over the coals or chew him/her out); ask questions; acknowledge employee difficulties, excuses, reasons and justifications when they come up (without bending over and letting the employee off the hook); own up to your share or contribution to the problems; and point out things that are going right. Once this has been done, you can gently start discussing Step 3.

STEP THREE:

ESTABLISH IMPACT

Think of Step 3 as the lubricant for the slow-moving gears of change. This step explains why the employee should consider revising his/her action or approach. Step 3 is a vital transitional step in moving from the issue or concern to the forward-looking action and commitment steps. Step 3 is like a hinge or linking pin. Through Step 3 you start to develop the genuine and deep cooperation of the employee.

The intent of Step 3 is to help the employee fully assess and make value judgments about any adverse impact that his/her actions are having on personal goals, the organization's operations, or other individuals and co-workers. By asking the employee to step back from the situation and evaluate the adverse impact, or by clearly stating the negative effects of the employee's actions to this point, you are creating an imbalance, doubts, and disruptions in the employee's "mind set" about the value of the current course of action. The more this tension or questioning is self-created by the employee, the more interested and ready the employee will be to entertain a discussion of new or different alternatives. Step 3 is designed to create the self-motivation to sustain the change process. The energy essential to take action will result when the employee examines the situation and sees how actions are working counter to valued or desired goals, objectives, intentions, and results. This is a tension-raising and complacency-disturbing process that sparks the search for new plans and actions. A good analogy of how Step 3 works is when you look in the

Benefits (+)	Costs (-)

Complacency-Disturbing

87

mirror after you have over-indulged during a long holiday, and you discover an extra layer of flesh protruding from your body that must go. As a leader, you act as the mirror and facilitate the employee's discovery and awareness.

Look at Blind Spots

This step is crucial because often the employee has a blind spot or is unable to see the full range of effects of actions. With this step, the leader is simply trying to heighten the employee's awareness of the rest of the world (i.e., customers, top management, co-workers, the leader, careers, other departments, the bottom line, etc.). The best way for the leader to create the impact and employee self-awareness is to create a very vivid example, ask penetrating questions about the costs and benefits of the employee's current actions, or actually create an experience outside of the coaching discussion. These things could be done by engaging the employee in some role reversal with you, customers, or other departments. The leader can *ask* the employee to do a mental re-evaluation of his/her means to reach certain ends. The leader can make an assignment which will bring the employee into *direct contact* with the problem or issue (up close and personal). Once this comes into focus, the employee will want to forge on with a new course of action.

"The success or failure of the action plan is most often determined by this step."

Our survey data and firsthand observations strongly suggest that this step, more than any of the others, is neglected and avoided. We suspect that leaders underrate the value of some discussion in this area and are in a rush to get on with Step 4 and a plan, or they are not sure how to use this step to achieve its

88

full value.

When the leader has elected to engage the employee in a positive motivational or developmental coaching discussion, this step becomes a powerful solidifying or reinforcing step for behavior that is desired. The leader would simply focus on the positive impact the employees actions are having on themselves, the organization, or other people.

Managers are sometimes puzzled because this step seeks to create a "pinch" and some internal stress in an effort to unfreeze the employee's thinking and position on the issue raised by the leader. That may seem on the surface as very *non*-supportive. We want to be clear about this. We are not advocating psychological torture, nor are we suggesting that you lay a heavy "guilt trip" on the employee. There is a real choice here about how heavy you want to be. We highly recommend that you start with some questions and allow the employee to discover and see the impact. Your questions may seem obvious and redundant to you. . . ask them anyway, and get a feel for how the employee is assessing the situation. Your best hope in communicating support for the employee is to ask, listen, and add to what the employee says. After doing that, you can recap with some direct statements and clarify again that your primary aim is to help the employee learn and grow, despite the fact that some self-realization may be a bit painful at first. Remember, change is sometimes preceded by an abrupt awakening and discovery.

Change= awakening and discovery

STEP 4:

INITIATE A PLAN

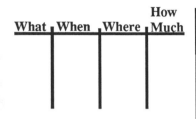

**Involve the
employee**

**Specific, simple,
clear, and
feasible**

Step 4 feels comfortable for most leaders because it sounds solid and positive. In fact, Step 4 is critical because it does represent "pay dirt," "the end zone," or the "bull's eye." Steps 1, 2, and 3 are the building blocks, but this is the place where the actual changes get worked out.

In this step the manager has a choice of creating and giving a plan to the employee or developing and *negotiating a plan* with the employee. Unfortunately, a lot of managers feel a strong need at this point to *take* control of the situation, dictate a plan to the employee, and then ask for a commitment to "the manager's" plan. We urge leaders to relax their need for control and to think of themselves as catalysts, organizers, and facilitators in jointly developing solutions *with* the employee, and not figuring out the solution for the employee. Obviously, the choice depends on the employee's ability and willingness to respond, and to really understand the impact of what's being done. If at all possible, the employee should be involved in making the plan. Using the employee's knowledge of the situation as well as his/her creativity and talent to develop a workable plan will help insure success. Remember that, from our study and research on this topic, collaboration is the highest form of support. So be as collaborative as the situation will allow if you want to build a partnership with your employee.

Regardless of who constructs the plan, it needs to be specific, simple, clear, and feasible; in addition, it needs to have timetables. In short, once the discussion on Step 4 has ended, the leader and employees need to be able to say who will do what, where, when, and how much.

Goals need to be set and clearly understood. Numerous studies have found that clear, difficult, specific goals work better than vague, easy-to-achieve goals. The manager needs to take the lead in making sure clear goals are established, because it is hard for an employee to hit a target that hasn't been set. Then, as much as possible, the manager should encourage the employee to provide ideas on how to reach the goals. The more input from the employee on the plan, the more likely the employee will feel part of the plan and will have ownership for results. As an outgrowth of working together, the employee's personal credibility and judgment, as well as the manager's, are on the line. This will help insure that the plans are fulfilled.

Set goals

"You can't hit a target that you don't set."

A lot of managers assume that if they have given the employee clear feedback in Step 2, and if they have helped the employee assess the impact from all the different angles, then the employee can construct a specific action plan alone. This is a dangerous assumption. Regardless of who comes up with the plan, the manager has the responsibility to insure that clear plans are in place. Specific actions must have been laid out, and clear timetables established.

91

STEP 5:

GET A COMMITMENT

**Employee's
intentions**

Once a plan has been defined, it is easy to make the mistake of not following through and soliciting clear intentions from the employee, of not articulating and literally asking for a commitment. By using clear and pointed words and questions, the manager is looking for a response from the employee that indicates a willingness and obligation to respond positively, that reveals ownership and responsibility, and that shows the employee does truly believe that the plan can be accomplished as constructed. Therefore, this step is designed to "lock up" a commitment to try the plan.

An employee may feel that the manager is encroaching on his/her freedom. Leaders may need to clarify to the employee that the intent is not to encroach, but to clearly understand and solidify the employee's intentions. It is important to be persistent, to get a clear answer, and to hear the employee actually verbalize a commitment. The manager simply cannot assume or hope that things will change and that plans will be implemented.

This step, then, is designed to tie it all together. It's a way to close the deal. Step 5 doesn't take a lot of time. It does take some courage on the manager's part to ask for commitment and to be clear in letting the employee know you are serious.

Some people ask why Steps 4 and 5 are not combined. The reason is that in our research we found that many managers assume that a commitment is there because a plan was built.

92

CHAPTER 3

THE 8 - STEP MODEL

Failure to gain a commitment often makes the difference between success or failure. We have kept this step separate in order to give it appropriate emphasis.

The key in Step 5 is to get a commitment and to initiate the first and most elementary step of the plan *immediately*. Don't let the employee sit around. When the employee leaves the meeting with you, he/she should be doing some positive act, regardless of its size, that will get the ball rolling. There are a thousand ways to ask for a commitment: "Will you try it?" "What do you think?" "Can you get behind this plan?" "When can you start?" "What could be done right now to begin?" "Do you think this will work?" It doesn't work to *tell* the employees to be committed. This has to be voluntary; you need to *ask* for it. The employee's response will give you vital clues regarding your need to monitor. The commitment step will signal any hesitation and whether the employee is saying "I can't" (due to a lack of knowledge, skill, or ability) or "I won't" (because of a belief that the plan won't work or because of a lack of motivation to change).

"The test of your work is whether the employee does something."

Ask for it

93

STEP 6:

CONFRONT EXCUSES/RESISTANCE

If applied incorrectly, this step could be interpreted by the employee as non-supportive. The main thrust is for the manager to convey a real determination to act on the plan without being insensitive, harsh, or unreasonable. The *firm* part of this step is trying to say to the employee that inactivity simply is not accepted. The *supportive* part of this step is trying to say it is okay to have excuses and reservations and to express them to a leader who will listen and work with the employee to solve them. In designing the model, this step was difficult to place in the 8-step wheel because excuses can develop at any point in the interaction process. However, as we did more investigating, we found that managers need to take two kinds of excuses into account. The first usually occurs as a result of discussion on Step 2, "Define the Topic and Expectations." Those excuses are designed to justify why things are happening the way they are. Although these can be distracting or annoying, they really don't do a lot of harm since they are part of the *past*. We refer to these excuses as Type I excuses.

"It's not my fault."
"It doesn't apply to me."
"No one told me."
"I didn't mean it. I was just practicing."

Type I Excuses

Type II Excuses

The other kind of excuse is that which surfaces when *future* plans and actions are being discussed. These excuses are the ones that create real problems for managers. For that reason, we place this step right after the planning and commitment step. These Type II excuses can submarine or threaten the plan and interfere with future progress.

Some people have a little trouble understanding why such a step should be

94

necessary once a commitment has been made. We have found that when there is hesitation, resistance, or a weak commitment to the plan, managers usually begin to see excuses develop at this point in the discussion. Some resistance or excuses are normal, natural, and to be expected when seeking a change from the employee. If the employee is placed in a new situation or asked to try new plans and approaches, the change has the potential of creating a sense of exposure or feelings of being out of control.

Because these kinds of excuses develop as a result of planning and commitment seeking, they pose serious *potential* threat to the action plan. The challenge here is to get the discussion back on track and moving in a positive, forward direction. The job of the manager is *not* to focus on the excuse, but rather to get the employee to focus on positive actions, contingencies, or back-up plans if problems materialize.

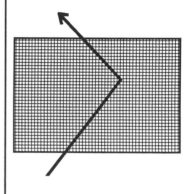

Excuses can be helpful

Point out that in some instances excuses can be helpful. They can provide an opportunity for the manager and the employee to foresee problems and do better contingency planning. The hope is that the manager can redirect the employee's thoughts and energy into realistic plans that aren't prone to obstacles and excuses. We strongly suggest that, even if it looks like the employee isn't going to offer any excuses or resistance, the leader take initiative with this step. The leader can do this by going on the offensive and literally *asking* the employee about any reservations regarding the plan. If the answer is *no*, this can be pursued further by asking the employee to anticipate or foresee any possible obstacle or reason that the plan might not work, and to suggest steps that could be taken now to prevent these conditions from occurring.

Managers shouldn't get bogged down in debates and arguments with their employees. The key is to get some constructive change started. If there are excessive excuses, one approach might be to simplify the plan. The manager should convey the expectation for change to occur and for cooperation from the employee, even if it means reducing the size of the plan.

Since excuses and resistance are mechanisms to insulate the employee from dealing with a harsh reality that requires a change, give the employee some support and indicate that you know it's difficult. Tell your employees that they are talented, you have faith in them, you are willing to support them, and you do expect some change to happen.

Focus on what can be done

The task of the manager in this step is to get the employee to focus less on excuses and reasons why things *won't* work and more on what *can* be done. Talk about what is within the influence and control of the employee, what bits and pieces are controllable. The manager can ask the employee what he/she can contribute in a constructive vein, what he/she is willing to do. The employee needs to see that the manager intends to confront resistance and excuses and is not willing to accept inactivity.

Inactivity is not accepted

If Steps 1 through 5 are done well, it's not likely that a lot of excuses will emerge.

96

STEP 7:

CLARIFY CONSEQUENCES, DON'T PUNISH

Step 7 creates some unique dilemmas or concern for the leader. First of all, during a conversation about performance, the manager wants to be clear without being overbearing about the outcomes for the employee if a plan is or is not implemented. Second, our research supports the idea that positive consequences have more impact than negative ones. Third, the manager needs to know when the consequences being discussed are viewed as punishment.

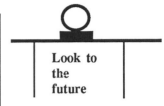

Look to the future

Positive consequences have more impact

Of all the 8 steps, "Clarifying Consequences" represents a dual-edged sword. One edge, the appropriate edge, will result in the employee clearly understanding the outcomes and in a solidification of the employee's commitment to give the agreed-to plan a valiant try. The other edge, the punitive side, will result in feelings of resentment and resistance from the employee, together with the recognition that the manager's power and authority--and not the employee's commitment--are the critical drivers for the plan.

IDEAS:

Use discretion

To help the manager stay on the appropriate edge, we offer the following ideas. First, use Step 7 with some discretion. The key is to assess the strength of the employee's commitment. If it is weak, the employee needs to understand the negative outcomes that will automatically occur if the plan fails. If it is strong, either forget the negative consequences or mention a few positive outcomes that the employee will experience by succeeding with the plan. Oftentimes this whole step can be omitted because the

97

manager and employee have developed a plan that has elicited the commitment and effort required to make it succeed.

Emphasize the positive

Second, emphasize the positive. The research suggests that positive consequences have a higher impact than negative consequences. This may seem to go against common sense--don't you get better results by scolding your children? But negative consequences were found to "repel" while positive consequences were found to attract the employee into wanting to give the plan an honest chance for success.

Focus on natural outcomes

Third, try to describe the consequences as natural outcomes that anyone could expect to occur as a result of doing or not doing the plan. These are really natural conditions like laws of nature or society. Don't let the employee think that he/she has been singled out for special negative or positive consequences. For example, any sales person who fails to meet with key decision makers can expect to close fewer sales and have lower sales commissions. These are natural consequences, not unique to any one person. If the person you are coaching doesn't accept or agree with the natural consequences, then you need to describe those that you as a leader can *impose* administratively (types of job assignments, performance ratings, salary adjustments, training opportunities, etc.). These imposed consequences represent the heavy artillery in coaching and should be used judiciously.

Fourth, as in Step 3, those consequences that are relative to the employee's personal goals or objectives carry more motivational weight than administrative consequences that can be imposed by the manager.

Relate them to personal goals

Keep this step in perspective. It is critical when you need to increase the employee's commitment and add motivational incentives to the plan. Don't use the negative consequences if they are not needed. Use positive consequences as often as you can, and keep them genuine. If the issue doesn't get resolved after the first or second coaching attempt, then you will want to increase the intensity and clarity of this step. The employee needs to know where he/she stands on the "playing field" and how close that is to being "out of bounds." This step is designed to be informational so that if, later on, it becomes necessary to administer the consequences the employee won't feel "ambushed" or surprised by the leader's actions. The good news about Step 7 is that it works. The bad news is that it is potent and you can "overkill" with it.

STEP 8:

DON'T GIVE UP

During the meeting

Think of this step occurring in two different time frames. The first is during the conversation with the employee, and the second is after the meeting.

During the meeting, this step illustrates your commitment to the employee. You have asked the employee to commit to a plan of action. Your commitment is to discuss and work through the other seven steps with the employee until both of you are comfortable. This means that you must trust the process and have the "supportive-toughness" not to let either yourself or the employee off the hook until all seven steps have been fully discussed, or a plan established as to when the remaining steps will be covered. Two excellent leader behaviors illustrate your attention to this step. One is to establish a precise date, time, and location to meet again and follow up on progress. The other is, during the final stages of the meeting, to take the initiative to verify, rehearse, or review one final time the next steps that the two of you will be taking.

A frequently asked question is how long you work with the employee or when it is okay to give up. An answer that is hard to quantify but serves as a useful guideline is *"longer than the employee expects you to."* Employee resistance to execute the plan or hesitation to talk openly about any one of these steps may in fact be a test--"Are the motives of this manager sincere and honest?" "Does my manager really care and want to spend the time it will take to help me change?"

You have to, through your persistence and actions, indicate that you are committed to solving this problem with the employee. So ask those additional questions or make those additional statements when you feel the most frustrated and want to call the meeting to an end. It will only take a few extra minutes and could send the strong message that you are serious and that the employee is not going to get around discussing this as easily as has been done in the past.

The commitment takes courage and patience, plus a willingness to devote the time. A lack of willingness to devote the time may indicate that the problem is not that important to you-- there are few quick fixes.

After the session, your follow-up actions become an important indicator of your willingness not to give up. It is interesting that in our research, employees more than managers desired extra contact to discuss their performance. Employees predicted that this would have a positive impact on their productivity. On the other hand, they felt their managers were reluctant to engage in these discussions either on an initial or continual basis. The highly effective coaches we studied had more frequent contact with their employees to discuss their performance than did the less effective coaches.

After the meeting

The question that needs pondering is how accessible and available you are to review progress and change the agreed-to plan after the employee gains some experience with trying to implement it. Our observations have been that, with the press of time, it is a common practice that once a problem has been discussed, it is assumed to be solved-- other things demand attention. This may be an additonal obstacle the employee sets up to test your commitment. "Will you follow up, or can I ignore our agreements because you won't bring them up again?"

The message is clear: if you invested the time and energy in getting the employee to understand the problem and plan a course of action, you need to invest some definitive time for follow-up. These follow-up sessions are often the most valuable because now it is you and the employee discussing the plan and how to make it work better, or how to make the partnership work better. The focus is on renewing commitments and revising plans, and away from the employee. All your good work and intentions could be wasted for the want of a series of brief review meetings to evaluate progress or needed changes.

CHAPTER 3

THE 8 - STEP MODEL

SUMMARY

After the initial exposure to the coaching model, some leaders are a little bewildered and slightly puzzled at the idea of being a strong supporter of the employee and also knowing that they need to initiate a rigorous problem-solving discussion. Sometimes these contradictions drive us away and discourage us from learning how to manage the apparent contradiction. The same is true in leadership. The effective leader supports and empathizes with an employee and then presses on with the process and initiates the problem solving. The effective leader has the ability to be firm and fair, to push at the right time, and yet be flexible at the appropriate moment. These themes are really embedded in our data and reinforce the support-initiate concept in coaching.

We challenge leaders to look closely at this coaching model. On the surface it may appear that we are asking the leader to do two opposing strategies (be kind...then stick it to them) or to do a sandwich technique (first some good news, next some bad news, then cap it with some more good news). These techniques represent manipulation and deception in its pure form. We believe that the leader's approach can be deeply genuine and needn't come across as a mixed or confusing message. The "support-initiate" model simply suggests that change in employee behavior is born out of your ability to be caring and interested, and the need to have a role in guiding and directing employee efforts. At times there will be conflict when organizational needs interfere with or limit the flexibility and freedom of individuals.

Apparent contradiction?

The challenge

"Remember, each coaching session is an opportunity to act out the type of partnership you want to create."

103

However, if you trust the process outlined here, you will be able to work through difficult times.

CHAPTER 4

SUPPORTING SKILLS

A. THE FAULT FACTOR

*"Everyone is **responsible**...and no one is to blame."*

"Don't blame me" is the most popular game in corporate America these days. The safest path is to avoid ownership for mistakes or omissions. This pattern can be observed among managers at all levels, as well as employees. It takes a lot of courage to admit mistakes, even if you have played only a contributing role. In truth, assigning fault or blame doesn't make a lot of difference if you agree with a forward-looking philosophy that advocates constructive action to deal with problems or to prevent them in the future. As mentioned earlier, employees clearly appreciate a leader who is willing to shoulder a fair share of the responsibility for problems. In fact, employees frequently attributed their cooperation and the success of coaching experiences to the leader's willingness to own up to his/her part of the problem and not pretend to be a paragon of virtue. Some research suggests that leaders who hold employees primarily and personally responsible for concerns or problems are likely to come down excessively hard on employees and create a barrier in the relationship (often referred to as a disaffiliative effect). Unfortunately, some leaders fear that owning a share of the problem looks like a sign of weakness and that the employee will play this up and sidetrack the whole coaching discussion. If you have read this far, you know that you can handle this perceived threat and keep the discussion focused.

Forward-looking philosophy

In reality, most problems and difficulties are caused by the interaction of many variables. Certainly the employee is a key factor in situations that involve his/her job or assignment. The leader also plays a part, either directly or indirectly, and like the employee's it is usually an inadvertent and unintended contribution. Sometimes leaders don't give clear assignments, define roles, or specify their expectations. Other contributing factors may include the organization's procedures, other units, and outside interference with the work such as government regulations, weather, equipment failure, communication breakdown, etc.

The contributors to problems

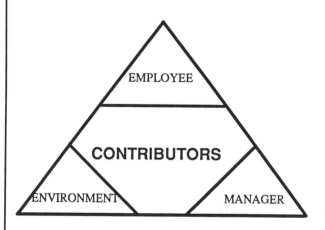

In most cases, many people and events contribute to the existence of problems and concerns. If you plan to launch a technical investigation, the most important challenge for the leader is not to be trapped in the vicious and non-supportive fault-finding game. This simply moves your actions away

CHAPTER 4

SUPPORTING SKILLS

from coaching. In some cases, a technical investigation and a detailed failure analysis may be appropriate. However, the coaching process is more concerned with establishing a course of action than with pathology. Please don't misunderstand. Analysis of cause can be an element of effective coaching, but it is not the main event. Focusing excessively on cause could be perceived and interpreted as a negative conversation and exchange by the employee. Remember, the main event is the creation of a *better vision of the future*. This means a clear direction, a jointly developed plan, and definite commitments to fix and prevent problems.

A better vision of the future

B. EMPLOYEES: ONE STEP AHEAD

"Don't shoot . . .we're on the same side."

Contrary to popular belief, the coaching session *is not* the beginning of the change process. Our studies and consulting indicate that, 90% of the time, employees already have a clue that a problem or challenge is on the horizon. Furthermore, some employees have already resolved to take action and correct an existing problem or prevent or minimize impending problems. This state of pre-existing readiness is called the employee's "own force" (self-motivation) for change. The trick for the manager in a coaching session is not to let employees feel too threatened, exposed, or vulnerable when they sit down with you. If employees believe that they won't be tortured or tormented, they will begin to relax and share data and impressions. Employees will naturally feel some initial anxiety and be a bit defensive, even when they are in safe hands. The manager can achieve a lot of success if he/she can tap into, heighten, and acknowledge the employee's own force or self-recognition of the situation.

"Own force"

Some leaders believe that the coaching session will help the employee who has perceptual blind spots by establishing the fact that a problem exists. However, the real challenge is to eliminate blind spots regarding the problem's "impact" and "consequences" of future action.

**Give employees
credit**

A common *omission* of leaders while conducting the coaching discussion is acknowledging and giving employees credit

CHAPTER 4

SUPPORTING SKILLS

for their awareness of the problem or concern, voluntary cooperation, and self-recognition of the needed change. After gathering research data on the coaching process from both leaders and employees, a fascinating pattern emerged. Leaders typically attributed their past coaching success to their own skillful orchestration of the coaching discussion. Employees, on the other hand, frequently attributed coaching success to their self-motivated effort to respond to change. Failure to understand that both the leader and employee play key parts in the coaching process can lead to serious complications.

From our experience, employees generally *don't* transmit graphic or extravagant verbal or non-verbal signs that they are attuned to the leader's line of thought and recognize that change is needed. It is as though the employee doesn't want to "let on" that the manager has a very good point which deserves serious consideration. That manager needs to be very alert and prepared to recognize and acknowledge a subtle yet positive shift of direction or recognition from the employee. The ability to put this into words is critical. For instance, if the employee says, "I guess I would be willing to give that a try," the leader could either assume that the employee is still not fully committed or that this represents some positive movement and respond by saying, "I am glad you are willing to try. It is important to be sure that you want to go ahead with this plan."

Managers need to be alert to subtle cues.

The objective of this procedure is to support the employee's internal willingness or

109

motivation to act constructively in the future. If the supervisor can recognize and reinforce the employee's "own force," then the ease and speed of the change will increase. One gets a dramatic sense of this phenomenon when listening carefully to *employee* accounts of previous coaching experiences. The following are word-for-word quotations from employees who have been interviewed:

Quotations from employees

-"I could see the nature of my supervisor's concern. I felt really bad about it. When these problems occur, they have a tremendous impact on our work."

-"Every error that is created results in an error for the company in terms of overpayments or underpayments."

-"I wanted to fix it as fast as my supervisor did. I knew that fixing this now would help me in the future."

-"My leader has a valid point. I probably had been wrong."

-"I was impatient. I wanted to correct it. If he had let this slide, it would have been a big problem later on."

Employees value expressions of appreciation in exchange for their support. If the leader doesn't acknowledge the employee's "own force" and treats the employee as though there were none, the employee may interpret the leader's actions as unnecessarily punitive or a "put-down." This may result from the leader overworking the issue or covering old ground from the employee's point of view. The leader simply needs to make sure that the

110

employee's awareness is *accurate* and the level of *readiness* is high enough, and then guide the employee into an action plan.

The goal in all of this is to let employees feel a part of the team, to recognize that employees have accurately detected the same concern or issue as the leader, and then to move the coaching process into the action plan. The bottom line is this: be prepared to give employees some credit. Look for the subtle signs that they are beginning to respond, and express your appreciation for their support and cooperation.

C. STYLE-"TO CONTROL OR NOT CONTROL"

**The amount of
press**

Communication style can be a confusing term. In coaching situations it is simply the level of intensity exhibited by the leader, or the amount the leader "presses," during each of the coaching steps. We contend that leaders can choose to be very direct or very indirect in pointing out the opportunities, concerns, plans, consequences, etc., to the employee.

**Start of less
direct**

Our findings indicate that in routine coaching situations (not emergencies), the best style for starting the coaching session is one that is less direct--more probing, questioning, and data gathering in nature. Any change in the leader's style should be justifiable. For example, if the employee fails to respond to the manager's flexibility and patience, the leader may use more direction and intensity to insure movement and progress toward the desired change and to complete the coaching steps. However, the risk is that moving up the intensity scale too fast may create unnecessary employee alienation and resentment.

Employees know when an issue or problem is brewing 90% of the time. Furthermore, they report that their cooperation and motivation to change or improve a situation are largely based on their ability to see the issue, realize its impact, and formulate new actions and plans without heavy or excessive control or direction from a leader. So a leader who is patient and backs away from the heavy control or press may avoid offending the employee and enable this natural ability within employees to operate.

112

If the employee doesn't initially respond to a low press style, the manager can test out a more direct and controlling style to complete the coaching cycle. A change in style works best, then, when a leader moves in a direction from lower to higher intensity or control. It is more painful, especially for the employee, to move from a high press or "pushing" style back to a low press or "pulling" style. The analogy can be made to running over the employee with a "Mack Truck" and then rushing in to rescue the employee when you find out it didn't take that much *punch!* It is hard to pick employees up, dust them off, apologize, and ask for their support after they have been hammered.

It's hard to move back to less direct

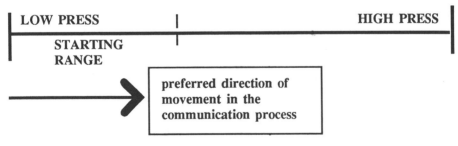

A lot of leaders ask us if it is okay to get tough with employees. We don't mind giving out permission slips to get tough if leaders have tried to resolve the issue using good-faith attempts to be supportive, patient, and honest. Frankly, some employees need direction and prescriptions. The key is not to handle all employees like that. The astute leader will know when to back off and create some psychological space or operating room

It's O.K. to use high press

for the employee and when it becomes necessary to press. You will probably need to vary your style between employees at different times and for different steps in the coaching model. By all means, if circumstances outside of your control are dictating the course of action, let the employee know this so your actions and intentions are not misinterpreted as aggressiveness, e.g., "Our timetable is short, so this has to be done this way or we're sunk." Just let them know that you want to work with them, utilize their abilities, and recognize their maturity and skill, when possible.

"The inclination to aggression...constitutes the greatest impediment to civilization."
--Sigmund Freud

D. BEING DESCRIPTIVE: ATTACK THE CONCERN NOT THE PERSON

The 8 steps can seem very confrontive to the employee, and you walk a tightrope at times and run the risk of sounding nonsupportive to the employee. Good coaching requires the leader to exchange views and perceptions about the problem at hand or opportunities available to the employee. The key to effectively managing and presenting information to the employee is "SDN" or Specific, Descriptive, and Non-Punishing. The art of being specific and descriptive is deceptively simple; the leader merely names and describes the employee's actions. For instance, if the employee is coming to work late, you can say, "I have noticed that you are checking in at 8:20." Or if the employee turns in a report late you can say, "I noticed that you turned in the report on the 10th rather than the 5th." The next step requires patience and silence. You just "hit the ball" into the employee's court. Let the employee respond, excuse, justify, or rationalize (all of which are normal and should even be expected; be prepared to tolerate and accommodate those expressions with empathy and without giving up on future solutions or corrective changes). By allowing the employee to express some views, you are giving him/her a chance to be heard, and you are demonstrating your willingness to interact and listen (key supportive skills). If the employee asks you whether the behavior you described is a problem, simply say "yes." That is enough. Then let the employee pursue his/her thoughts, vent, or explain further.

S.D.N.

Specific

Descriptive

Non-Punishing

115

THE COACH

How attack sounds

Unfortunately some leaders attack the person in a more forceful and nonsupportive fashion. The leader sounds more punitive when he/she says, "You are always late for work" or "Your report is late again, as usual." The motives behind these types of remarks are usually punishment, embarrassment, or getting even. The hope is that this *aggressive* approach will *force* the employee to change. Often the leader is acting out of highly charged emotions, anger, and frustration. These too are normal for leaders and counterproductive. They can best be handled with a little preparation time and by thinking descriptively about the behavior.

Fair, clear, objective

The "SDN" approach, on the other hand, is born out of the need to be fair, clear, and as objective as possible with the employee. Even with your best efforts, the employee may misinterpret your motives. If that seems to be happening, simply say that your intent is to be clear and not to blame, accuse, or "put the employee down." If you can learn to describe actions and performance as an engineer would describe a valve (facts, dimensions, specifications, etc.) without injecting emotionally charged innuendos, put-downs, or biased hints, you will create a starting point for the coaching session that will be constructive and less threatening to the employee.

116

E. PUTTING YOUR EXPECTATIONS TO WORK

Webster defines "boss" as one who exercises control or authority; one who directs or supervises workers.

A common notion is that leaders are the bosses and have the power and authority to make things happen with employees. Power can easily be intentionally or unintentionally abused or misinterpreted. We believe that leaders can effectively use indirect power and leverage and get better results than if they use aggressive, demanding, and controlling behavior. The art of using indirect leverage with employees lies in the power of clear *expectations*.

Indirect leverage lies in clear expectations

Employees and leaders have fascinated us by their incessant references to the role that clear leader expectations (goals) played in facilitating change in the employee's performance and how these aided the coaching success. In fact, from the data we gathered from leaders, employees, and real coaching discussions, expectations were probably the most dominant of the initiation or problem-solving behaviors.

Leaders had these comments in reference to expectations:

Examples

"I told him it was essential that the project be completed by the deadline."

"I told her I didn't want her to quit, and I needed her to be a team player."

"I said we must honor established organizational procedures."

"I explained to him that I needed to go over the reports before they were presented."

"I want accurate reports."

"I told her that it was unacceptable to not keep me informed when she was in trouble."

Employees had this to say:

"She said she needed everyone's full cooperation."

"He said failures like this should never happen again."

"My manager made it clear that if I had questions that I should ask."

"She said in this organization you have to be cost effective and still be considerate of customers."

"He told me to slowdown and be more analytical."

State what you want

A leader simply needs to state what he/she wants from the employee, listen to the employee's response, and then seek agreement and commitment to the goals and expectations. The purpose of this procedure is to enable the employee to say to anyone, "I know what my job is in this situation." We have found that leaders understate and underrate the power of expectations when, in fact, they should be prepared to state and restate expectations so the employee can gain a clear vision of the leader's direction. This process is much like a contracting process in

118

which wants and offers are exchanged.

It is tempting and time efficient for leaders to "bark out" orders and demands based on the authority and power of their positions. However, our data suggest that leaders simply need to clarify the *"end"* objectives and then give the employee an opportunity to develop and contribute by generating the *means* of achieving the ends. Expectations then take on the role of an employee "self-monitoring" mechanism, especially when the expectations are clear, understood, and accepted. Much evidence suggests that the expectations and goals be highly challenging in order to achieve the best results. Once the goals are in place, leaders can simply call attention to and keep the employee focused on them. Expectations allow the employee to do more "self management" and require less "bossing" by the leaders. Employees can do more self-evaluation, thus allowing the leaders to do less judging and criticizing.

More "self management," less "bossing"

THE COACH

F. QUESTIONS AND SILENCE

"Silence   is   the   most   underutilized communication tool!"

"Don't talk unless you can improve the silence."
--Vermont Proverb

This problem emerges over and over again: managers try to power their way through a difficult coaching situation with a monologue or lecture to the employee. It *is* appropriate for a leader to let the employee know what he/she is thinking and to keep the employee on track, but we also believe that questions and   measured   silence   are   underutilized techniques. For instance, a leader may want to *tell* the employee about the consequences of closing a large sale: "You know, Joan, that this sale means you will earn an extra $1,500 bonus." The other available option for the leader to make the same point is to encourage   the   employee   to   think   and articulate by asking *questions*: "Joan, how much bonus will this sale generate for you?" Even if the employee requires a little time to respond, a little silence allows the impact of your point to sink in. In fact, it is probably good if Joan has to figure out (with a pencil and paper) that this sale means a great deal to her.   Don't be afraid to use rhetorical or simplistic   questions   on   occasion.   For example, "What effect do you think this sale will have on your sales goal?" The point is simply this: questions and silence allow the employee to think and concentrate instead of just passively listening to you talk.   This approach enables the employee to actively

Allow the employee to think and discover

participate   in   the   discussion   as   well   as "discover." Questions and silence form the cornerstone   of   a   more   non-directive communication   and   coaching   style. Questions reveal what the employee does and

120

doesn't know. The silence, although awkward, punctuates your meaning and resolve in making a point.

The direct vs. indirect coaching styles are contrasted below. One style is not necessarily better than the other. We are simply suggesting that if you lean on one style too much, it gets repetitive and boring for the employee; that goes for the questioning technique too. The employee will at times want you to make direct statements. Illustration 4.1 may be helpful.

Illustration 4.1

INDIRECT STYLE	DIRECT STYLE
• Use wide-focus questions that avoid "yes" or "no" answers.	• Make clear and simple statements
• Listen to the employee's response, but move the discussion to specifics (narrow or funnel the discussion).	• Get to the point quickly
• Probe for suggestions and build on the employee's ideas.	• Don't soften the impact of the with excessive thoughts, explanations, or justifications.
• Restate key points	• Own your statements- Use "I" instead of "we" and "they" saw or said this or that.
• Bridge the gap and encourage more conversation ("I see," "Uh-huh," "Yes," "Tell me more about that," etc.)	• Use questions that narrow the focus of the discussion.
• Summarize and check for accuracy understanding	• Be sensitive and aware of resistance and withdrawal
	• Confront resistance--put it into words.
	• Plan to get more information if that's a concern

Sample questions

Here is a list of specific penetrating questions that can be used with the 8-step coaching model. These questions will help you gain critical information with a less direct style.

Step 1-"Are you getting enough support from me?"
   -"What can I do to help you be as successful as possible?"

Step 2-"What do you want to achieve with this project?"
   -"Where do you think we stand on this assignment?"

Step 3-"How will your current approach help you achieve your goals?"
   -"What are some of the risks with your current approach?"

Step 4-"What do you think we should try?"
   -"What will we do if that doesn't work?"

Step 5-"Are you really committed to this new plan?"
   -"When can you get started?"

Step 6-"Is it something you really want to try?"
   -"Is there anything you can anticipate that might get in our way or interfere down the road?"

CHAPTER 4

SUPPORTING SKILLS

Step 7-"From your point of view, what is riding on this plan?"
  -"Do you see how important this plan is?"

Step 8-"When can we meet next?"
  -"What do you want to start on first?"

"A prudent question is one-half of wisdom."
--Francis Bacon (1561-1626)

G. SURFACING UNDERLYING ISSUES

In our society we have grown accustomed to putting transactions in writing to signal our commitment and resolve. Even the computer age may contribute to an era marked by fewer face-to-face or one-on-one verbal interactions. Over time this trend may affect our verbal communication skills and leaders' ability to supportively confront important communication tasks such as delegating, coaching, and training employees. This potential problem could affect employees as well as leaders, thereby restricting and interfering with leader/employee interactions.

**Put it
into words**

The art of putting what you think, feel, or see into words is a deceptively simple skill. In fact, after working with thousands of managers in hundreds of companies, we have noticed that the most challenging skill is acting in an authentic and assertive way by effectively converting intentions, thoughts, and feelings into words. Countless times at the conclusion of a role play or a practice coaching session, we have asked why leaders didn't comment or draw attention to some painfully obvious and unavoidable resistance, difference, or misunderstanding. They answer by saying, "I saw it happening. It was crystal clear that the employee didn't believe me, but I didn't know what I should say or do about it," or " I am sure the employee thought I was being difficult or hardheaded about this issue, but I didn't know how to handle the employee's silence."

The most effective way of handling these situations is to clarify and state your intentions, specify the support you want to give, and articulate your expectations. Likewise, when you perceive resistance, reluctance, or misunderstandings, be prepared to go the extra mile and put your observations of the employee's behavior into *words*. Employees may have a hard time owning up to the fact that they disagree with the leader, and so their feelings show up later in the form of some underlying low-level resistance. In other situations, employees won't confess that the leader's feedback was painful or even devastating to them personally, and so we see the signs and aftermath in the form of defensiveness and argumentation or in the passive resistance, such as silence or giving in. If you feel the employee is giving in too easily, stimulate some conversation about it by saying, "You seem to be quite accepting of this," or "I expected you to debate this a little," or "So far you have agreed with everything I have suggested; somehow I am detecting that you are unsure about this." The key here lies in simply *describing* the physical signs, rather than interpreting and jumping to conclusions about what they mean. If you are patient, employees will take responsibility and clarify their reactions, emotions, and thoughts.

Describe the physical signs

This procedure not only clarifies your position but can also be used to "smoke out" the employee's honest reactions, thoughts, and feelings. The conversation becomes more genuine and authentic if you take the lead and signal to the employee that his/her honest reactions, interpretations, and feelings are vital to an effective conversation. This

125

Be silent

"To say the right thing at the right time, keep still most of the time."
--John W. Roper

procedure basically communicates to the other person that you value open, honest, and direct discussion. Once the leader has used words to draw some attention to the subtle indicators of the employee's reaction, then the next step is to be silent. This silence serves as a graphic shift of conversation and responsibility; it suggests that the employee express or amplify on your observations. This may make the employee uncomfortable, but if you get no response, repeat the process again. The tension you are creating, if not overdone, will create the urge in the employee to open up more to you. Silence, probably the most underutilized communication tool in this process, is critical. If the employee begins to disclose or "level" with you, even if only a little, be prepared to offer support for taking a risk and for telling you what he/she is really thinking and feeling. Remember, the clarity and authenticity that you are striving for are valued elements of the coaching discussion.

A. POSITIVE GAME PLAN

1. THE "ONE MINUTE" LEADER-- ONE BIG MYTH!!

From our data and observations, the pattern is strong and clear: highly effective leaders and successful coaching discussions consumed 40% more time than was spent by other leaders in unsuccessful coaching discussions. The evidence shows that 30 to 45 minutes is an appropriate timeframe for a fully developed coaching interaction.

"Employees will judge your supportiveness by your *actions* as well as your words."

30-45 minutes is needed

There is no question that leaders today are obsessed with saving time because they are under serious time pressures. Organizations require leaders to attend to a lot of routine administrative and sometimes bureaucratic activities such as budget reports, meetings, committees, community relations. In addition, they have a huge list of reading materials, in-baskets, and professional association responsibilities. The list is endless, and there simply is never enough time to do all that can or should be done. For this reason, it is easy for the leader to lose focus of what a leader really is: a manager of *people* and their performance, not a manager of paper, projects, equipment, money. Please don't misunderstand: the management of things is critically important to success in any organization. However, a common mistake that we have observed is that many managers end up taking time from their "leadership" responsibilities (coaching, directing, delegating, etc.) in order to meet other administrative responsibilities. Some managers have not received the training or

127

**Activity
trap**

don't have a vision of what leadership really is. They end up filling their days with other activities and, therefore, unintentionally minimizing or neglecting their leadership role and ending up like other managers in the "Activity Trap."

To address this problem, writers are proposing some tempting but dangerous options. For example, the "one minute" approach is being aggressively peddled to managers as a solution to time pressures. The basic idea is that you can reward, reprimand, or engage in other leadership functions literally in "one minute." This idea is obviously popular and appealing from a time management point of view. Frankly, we believe that it is preposterous to think or even try to do coaching in one minute. The reality is that, in terms of a meaningful and effective coaching session, the "one minute" notion is pure myth. In coaching employees about existing or potential performance concerns, career opportunities, or even positive performance, the leader cannot excessively rush the discussion if real employee support or "buy in" is desired. Obviously a number of factors cause the 30-45 minute guideline to increase or decrease. For instance, emergency situations, high levels of leader-employee agreement, clarity or simplicity of the solution, high level of employee experience, etc., suggest that the leader can be more time efficient. On the other hand, differences or conflict, low employee experience, ambiguity, personal sensitivity, complexity, etc., suggest a more thorough and expanded discussion. We also know that in some organizations, leaders have to supervise large numbers of employees (more than 8).

128

CHAPTER 5

THE COACH'S CONTRIBUTION
(positive game plan)

We encourage you to read the chapter on how time can be saved, without sacrificing quality, in a coaching session.

When a leader says, " I am prepared to take the time necessary for a high-quality discussion," the leader is indirectly supporting and saying to the employee, "I care about you, I care about this issue, I want to see you be successful, I care about your input and perceptions, and I want this concern resolved in more than a superficial way." Patience and courtesy in a coaching discussion are the basic fabric of supportiveness. Speeding up a discussion denotes a need to push or force the issue and may result in increased employee resistance. The bottom line is that a good coaching session is like a quality cheese; it takes more than a minute to develop into a quality product.

**I care enough
to spend the time**

2. DOING YOUR HOMEWORK

A critical difference distinguishes planning from worrying and agonizing about a pending coaching session.

Primary benefit

"How to's"

One of the most striking findings from our interviews with leaders and employees was the amount of emphasis given to planning and preparation prior to the coaching discussion. Effective leaders don't make elaborate plans, nor do they spend lengthy periods of time planning. However, they do collect accurate data, anticipate problems, and mentally rehearse key parts. Carried to an extreme, the planning stage can become a source of procrastination or an excuse for "putting off" the one-to-one problem solving. The primary benefit of planning appears to be its tendency to deflate the emotionally charged nature of some issues. Employees really pick up on the leader's level of preparation, the accuracy of data, and the extent that the leader is emotional, overly aggressive, or impatient.

So what does a leader do in order to really prepare for the discussion? Well, here is a plan that we have developed from working with highly successful leaders.

I. THE GROUNDWORK

1. In your own mind, define and articulate your expectations and the mission of the employee as soon as possible. You might pretend that you are trying to explain these to a "new" employee as a way of checking for clarity.

130

2. Develop an accurate description of the situation you wish to discuss. Base the description on facts that can be supported.

3. Write down a few of the key words you plan to use. Ask yourself if they are clear, supportive, and focused on problem solving. Some words may seem very volatile and highly charged to the employee. Try to avoid these.

4. Good questions can be more effective than statements, so write down two or three central questions to help the employee think about the situation and to stimulate involvement in the discussion. Try to anticipate any blind spots or things that the employee may be unaware of, and consider how you can illustrate your perceptions and increase awareness.

II. THE DELIVERY

1. Be prepared to level with the employee. It isn't uncommon for leaders to be afraid of hurting the feelings of an employee who is typically a good performer. The dilemma is that you will hurt the employee's feelings more and lose his/her respect for you as a leader if you don't "shoot straight."

2. Think through your contribution to the situation. We haven't seen a case yet where the leader didn't play some role. No doubt the outcome was unintended and not totally your fault either, but you can win a lot of points in the employee's mind if you accept your fair share of responsibility.

THE COACH

3. What types of actions and commitments from the employee would represent a fair beginning with respect to resolving this concern? Don't go overboard and define the entire solution. . .give the employee a little space and a chance to collaborate and build up some ownership in terms of the solution. Remember, we found wide agreement that collaboration is the highest form of support and respect you can show to the employee. What other types of supportive statements can you make that the employee will value and respond to?

III. REACTIONS

1. Anticipate and program yourself to react as objectively as possible if your views are challenged. Remember, because you are, in effect, examining and questioning the employee's behavior, the employee may become defensive and feel exposed, which is normal and natural. . .don't take the hostility personally.

2. Plan to listen to the employee's reactions. What does he/she want you to hear? Usually employees feel trapped and victimized by circumstances. It is okay to show some empathy without calling off the problem-solving process.

FOR ADDITIONAL HELP IN PLANNING FOR THE DISCUSSION, SEE:

THINKING IT THROUGH-- PLANNING GUIDE (IN THE APPENDIX)

"Nothing is more terrible than activity without insight."
--Thomas Carlyle (1795-1881)

132

3. ATTENDING TO EARLY WARNING SIGNALS

When leaders explain their problems in managing employee performance, we invariably detect that the leaders saw clear indications of the problems emerging well before the situations ever became critical or unavoidable. Employees are also frequently aware of the signs that indicate trouble ahead. Perhaps the signals were not strong enough to be conclusive, or perhaps the leader was unable to muster up sufficient courage to confront a relatively minor situation.

"You don't have to be psychic, just very observant, in order to head off a disaster."

In focusing on the topic of early warning signals, we simply suggest that a leader act like radar and *not* ignore "blips" on the screen. "Light," or non-directive, coaching designed mainly to gather information, check the employee's direction and progress, clarify a task, or remind an employee of something to be considered, is not scary or dangerous work. In fact, this style of coaching fits in nicely with a *regular* pattern of healthy and non-threatening (planned) contacts and meetings with the employee. This way everyone knows that the scanning or "radar detection" is just as predictable as in an airport control tower.

Watch the blips

We have assembled a list of generic early warning signals that have emerged from our consultations with leaders. If any of these conditions are occurring in your day-to-day operations, the signals will emanate externally from the employee, or you will feel them internally (psychological or physiological) in your head, stomach, tight fists, or various other extremities. These signals indicate a need for exploratory coaching which is less tense, less risky, and more proactive in nature.

MANAGEMENT'S EARLY WARNING SIGNALS OF POTENTIAL PROBLEMS/OPPORTUNITIES

A check list

Look over this check list carefully, and see if any of these conditions occur in your day-to-day supervision of this employee.

EMPLOYEE SIGNALS

-falls behind and delays progress on assignments
-has very vague action plans and strategies for the future
-has no specific target completion dates for key assignments
-has grossly optimistic estimates and expectations for assignments
-submits reports that are increasingly late
-shows no initiative to communicate and account for personal results
-conducts infrequent visits and updates with the leader
-overlooks or forgets important matters
-forgets to return phone calls
-becomes defensive in response to your questions and inquiries
-tries overselling you on substitutes or shortcuts
-lacks attention or concentration to detail

-shows a change in enthusiasm level
on assignments
-shows an increase in absenteeism or
preoccupation with personal matters
-makes promises and exaggerations
that are unreal
-rarely expresses voluntary
commitment
-rushes too fast to get things done at
the last minute
-focuses on excuses and justifications
for mistakes
-makes requests for unusual
extensions in deadlines
-continually misunderstands your
instructions
-relies too much on the manager for
ideas and direction
-creates in-fighting or conflicts with
other group members

MANAGER SIGNALS

-feels disappointment
-discovers unexpected surprises
-has feelings of uncertainty
-experiences tension and worrying
-constantly second guesses the
employee
-over-rationalizes, hoping and
wishing for "luck"
-feels confusion
-gives in too much

"Ignorance is no
excuse--it's the
real thing."
--Irene Peter

SEVEN PIECES OF THE PERFORMANCE PUZZLE

Don't just attribute it to the employee

Other possibilities

Once a leader observes a problem or senses that an issue needs to be discussed with an employee, the leader should consider its possible causes. It is common (well documented in other studies) for leaders to excessively attribute the cause to the employee (especially when the issue bears directly on the leader's own performance). We hear leaders say the employee just isn't motivated, committed, or talented enough. While these factors do frequently contribute to problems, we have found that the astute leader examines other contributing factors or characteristics before coming down hard and singling out the employee as the culprit. We have identified and defined seven common characteristics of the situation that could contribute to creating the circumstances faced by the leader and employee in the coaching session.

1. **Employee motivation, willingness, or desire:** When this appears to be a contributing factor, the leader needs to work at raising the employee's felt need for change or at disturbing the employee's complacency (Step 3). In addition, the leader can point out or draw attention to consequences of fulfilling a plan of action (Step 7). As far as Step 4 is concerned, the leader should make sure the employee's role in the solution is challenging, interesting, and inherently rewarding.

2. **Employee knowledge, skill, or ability:** If this is playing a role in creating or sustaining the situation, the leader needs to

136

consider formal training, guided practice, or feedback on results of the employee's efforts. Remedies can be built into the plan of action (Step 4).

3. **Employee personality match with the job and organization:** If a mismatch exists, and employees are too dependent on leaders or tend to be nonconformist to the point of disruption, then the leader either needs to encourage the employee towards more risk taking as part of the action plan or to seek alternative job settings or job structures to insure a more compatible and satisfying situation (all of this is part of Step 4).

4. **Employee "blind spots" or lack of awareness:** Sometimes the employee is unattentive to performance signals and yardsticks, or they are not available to guide the employee's performance. This simply requires more feedback on progress (Step 2), and putting signals and indicators in place to help employees help themselves in the future (Step 4).

5. **System obstacles, or organizational policies and procedures:** Sometimes the employee encounters cumbersome policies or procedures that interfere with performance. Other departments or individuals can also create logjams in moving an assignment along. The solution lies in creative alternatives, calculated risks, and back-up plans (Step 4).

6. **Resources:** When time, dollars, equipment, and people are tight, employees

experience frustration and lower productivity. Either expectations and standards need to be adjusted (Step 2), or plans for more efficient utilization of resources will have to be developed (Step 4).

7. Communication breakdown:
Confusion and misunderstanding about priorities, roles, responsibilities, or estimates can create interference and greatly impact employee production.

Leaders need to be sensitive to these seven general areas and prepared to direct the discussion and the coaching steps in a way that will address the key contributing causes. This will help balance responsibility for the problem and prevent exceeding the employee's willingness or ability to perform. Our data suggest that the bigger the problem, the more likely a leader is to focus on the employee's motivation and skill. This creates defensiveness and resistance, and ultimately a severe stress on the relationship and on trust. This backfire effect can be avoided by fairly allocating responsibility for the problem. This doesn't mean letting the employee off the hook. It simply means directing the coaching discussion (information gathering, plans, commitments, etc.) to those contributing factors that will most help to solve the problem.

CHAPTER 5

THE COACH'S CONTRIBUTION
(positive game plan)

5. FOCUSING ON FORM VS. SUBSTANCE

During the data-collection phase of our study, an interesting pattern emerged. The leaders we talked to usually selected a coaching experience in which the employee's "form"--communication skills, relationships, or individual style--was the central concern. When we talked to employees, they shied away from exposing personal issues and focused instead on "substance"--task-related problems and performance of the job itself (in other words, quality, errors, or technical difficulties in "what" they did rather than process issues or problems in "how" they did their jobs).

"Working with people is difficult, but not impossible."
--Peter Drucker

This finding lends some credence to the argument that nontechnical or personal issues are more sensitive and perhaps more difficult to discuss because of the personal exposure for the employee. Furthermore, leaders seem to be saying that these issues are extremely relevant and important. It may be that employees underrate the significance of these aspects of their performance. They assume that if the job itself is done well, that's all the manager should care about. Therefore, leaders should be prepared to be as descriptive and precise as possible when bringing up these more subjective topics that are hard to measure. Perhaps leaders need to openly admit to employees that these are difficult, ambiguous, and yet vitally important topics. It will be helpful to the leader to think about examples and demonstrations, and to be able to point to others who seem to have mastered the subtleties of the job.

Personal issues are more sensitive

THE COACH

Expect resistance

Leaders are likely to encounter employee resistance to changing personal habits and styles that may have been acceptable in the past or at least not objectionable to the employee. These days, growth, and especially upward or lateral career mobility, depends less on proving technical competencies and more on demonstrating leadership skills (social, positive, political). Employees need coaching and clarification from leaders that total effectiveness entails more than mere efficiency in performing the basic job. This is a dramatic revelation to many employees. Improvement may require gentle persistence on your part, and certainly results will be slower to develop and less detectable than in the more quantifiable area of job productivity.

6. THE OVERLOAD PROBLEM

Once leaders have built up the courage to confront employees in a constructive dialogue, their tendency is to overload or "dump" too many issues on the employee. Because many issues may have built up, once leaders have the employee in a coaching session, they like to "clear the deck" of all of the issues. This creates pressure that has to be managed in a patient or disciplined way. If the leader opens the floodgates of unresolved issues, he/she runs the risk of sounding punitive and resentful rather than solution oriented. Nearly 75% of the employees that we talked to during our research indicated that they would prefer leaders who focus on one or two issues at most in a coaching discussion. Keep in mind that "individual differences" do enter the picture because a few "hardy souls" (approximately 10%) of the employees preferred that leaders hold no issues in reserve.

Focus on one or two issues

Now that the leader is meeting the employee face to face, it seems, on the surface, that the natural and mature thing to do is just lay all the cards on the table. However, if the leader is really focused on the coaching process, then the availability of time and energy dictates that only one, or two issues at most, be discussed and resolved as fully as possible. Simply put, most employees have a finite capacity or threshold that enables them to focus, absorb, and remember limited amounts of information and plans generated during the coaching session. By dumping on employees, you rob them of the hope and motivation that you want to create in order to

Stay focused

141

change things in the future. This is one reason why employees get frustrated in the annual performance appraisal when so many topics and so much performance have to be discussed.

Remember, the goal of a coaching session is to make the employee comfortable in working through one issue with you in a routine and relatively informal process. Furthermore, you stand a better chance of creating a positive "snowball" effect if you can establish a pattern of success with one issue. Be cautious if the employee urges you to "unload." He/she may be trying to prove to you the capability of handling a lot of feedback rather than of doing something about the issues. If the employee wants to turn the coaching session into a dumping session, take a firm stand about putting a cap on the issue. Indicate that from time to time you would like to discuss other relevant issues, but for this time period you believe it is important to focus on the one concern that has been raised. Tell the employee that you recognize that other issues are important; then ask when a good time would be to talk some more. Thank employees for their assistance and contribution regarding the initial concern, and wish them sincere good luck on their action plans.

CHAPTER 5

THE COACH'S CONTRIBUTION
(winning mental attitude)

B. WINNING MENTAL ATTITUDE

1. THE DILEMA OF THE INHERITED EMPLOYEE

Imagine that your boss just handed you a fat promotion. That's the good news. The bad news is that your new assignment is to head up a unit that has been struggling for two years. Your boss graciously relieved the previous manager with these unsettling words, "I don't know how we are going to get along without you, but starting Monday we are going to try!" Realizing that this dilemma has created some mixed motivations, we made sure that the good witch of the North happened along and granted you three wishes for your unit. What would yours be?

Three wishes

We will refund the purchase price of this book if you didn't include the freedom to build your own staff of employees. But, in reality, you will end up working with some employees who are already in place. Will your approach be different for these two groups of employees? Most of us would like to believe we would treat everyone equally and consistently. However, the information we have gathered suggests that managers treat *inherited employees* differently than voluntarily *selected employees*. We call this phenomenon the "inheritance effect." Managers tend to affiliate with employees they select or hire, and disaffiliate with those employees they inherit as part of an existing organization.

The inheritance effect

The relationship is more often perceived by both managers and employees as positive and supportive when employees are hired by the manager. For inherited employees,

Support is harder when you didn't hire them.

143

THE COACH

establishing a supportive relationship can be more difficult, and a critical, pessimistic climate may prevail. In fact, the leader may attribute problems in the organization to the existing work force and be instantly critical of employee performance. The "inheritance effect" represents the difference between the known and the unknown. The leader knows the limits and capabilities and the extent the known employee can be trusted; the leader counts on this employee's support. For those employees who were already on board in the organization, the employee may be a little "suspicious" until the employee proves himself/herself over and over again.

Self-fulfilling prophecy

With regard to coaching situations, this mind set results in a self-fulfilling prophecy: When asked to describe negative coaching situations, 70% were with employees the manager inherited. Two-thirds of the positive coaching situations were with employees the manager hired. Managers found it a pleasure to coach and counsel those employees they hired. We believe this is due to a feeling of loyalty, a need to develop those hired, and a desire to validate the correctness of the original selection decision. For inherited employees, the manager is more critical; and with a lack of a positive, supportive relationship, the counseling sessions can more easily turn out to be negative or punitive, or the manager can come on too strong.

How to overcome this

The following are some suggestions to help overcome the inheritance effect:

1. List the positive and negative behaviors you associate with each employee working

144

for you. For those employees that you inherited, do the negatives outweigh the positives, or are there some serious concerns on the list? If so, and you don't feel good about this conclusion, continue.

2. For each inherited employee, analyze if the listed negative behaviors are based on your own actual observations, assumptions from the past, or hearsay evidence?

3. For those negative behaviors based on assumptions, define a way of assessing if these are truly negative behaviors or just a function of your disaffiliative mind set. Some examples include work projects, discussions with the employee, or an honest reassessment on your part.

4. To reverse the self-fulfilling prophecy, establish a course of action that you initiate to build a positive relationship with your inherited employees. Actions include the following:

    a. Get to know these people better.

    b. Make sure that they know that you are a supportive leader (clarify this with them).

    c. Don't tackle too many issues or concerns at once.

    d. Be extra sure that you have supporting data if you do have a concern.

    e. Give them recognition and acknowledge their contributions.

f. Try to conduct positive and motivational coaching sessions. (See the chapter on this topic).

Exercise patience

The main thing that we are trying to suggest in this section is that the leader needs to exercise a little extra precaution when coaching the inherited employee. To put it simply, the leader may not perceive these employees as positively as those selected, and the employee may detect a hint of hostility, unless you pay extra attention to supportive behaviors.

2. THE COURAGE AND THE AGONY OF COACHING

Coaching an employee on a sensitive and personal topic like performance or contribution to the organization can be as difficult and agonizing as telling a young son or daughter about "sex." You end up playing the same mental games in your head over and over again: "What should they be told? How much do they already know? (Or how much do they want me to think they know?) How much detail do I go into?" When you are unable to answer these penetrating questions, you put the task off for another six months. Eventually you discover the harsh reality that there is very little they are unaware of, but a lot they don't know.

Nearly everyone feels uncomfortable when coaching employees, yet few are willing to admit that they feel ambivalent or not fully adequate. Many leaders who say, with some pride, that they have no hesitation tend to approach the job like a bulldozer (overly aggressively). In fact, coaching is risky (you may lose control of the situation), and you are vulnerable (you have to substantiate your case, and your leadership style may be questioned by the employee). Consequently, you exaggerate your worst fears, you get uptight, you worry the night before the discussion is to take place, and you try to figure out ways to avoid or postpone it. But deep down, you know this isn't a helpful strategy.

Most of us favor directness, candor (trust), and honesty, as well as efficiency, excellence, and quality. But these goals cannot be met unless leaders are more willing

"We must have courage to bet on our ideas, to take the calculated risk, and to act. Everyday living requires courage if life is to be effective and bring happiness."
--Maxwell Maltz

Everyone feels
uncomfortable

147

to set aside ambivalence and hesitation, and to trust that the skills and ideas presented in this book will work.

Rationalization

Many leaders rationalize that the issue or concern isn't worth the time or effort of a coaching session. But this comes back to haunt them later when the employee's work is put under the microscope of others (their boss, customers, regulatory agencies, etc.). This occurs when a new position is to be filled that is an advancement for the employee, at performance appraisal time, and during the crucial high-exposure stages of an important project. At these times, earlier hesitation ends up costing both the leader and the employee very directly.

Why leaders resist the discussion

We have heard many explanations and rationalizations about why leaders resist speaking with employees more frequently about progress and problems. The reality is that no one wants to hurt people or jeopardize their performance in areas that are meeting or exceeding expectations. Leaders go about insulating themselves from facing the reality that a meaningful discussion will help improve things. So leaders:

-*hope* for a miracle, that things will get better without any intervention.
-*pray* that the employee will gain some enlightened self-awareness.
-*worry* that any action or discussion will only make matters worse.
-*rationalize* or discount the concern by taking other things (areas of
  successful performance) into account.
-*believe* that they can hobble along and get by

148

with minimal damage.

-*fret* that the issue will get escalated or that the employee will resent them and attack back.

-*painfully* realize that they have made mistakes too and have little right to be pointing the finger at others. This puts leaders in an awkward position when they advocate changes and improvements in others (the ill-equipped-judge syndrome).

-*feel* doubts about their own ability to orchestrate and guide a really productive discussion (especially if emotions enter the picture).

Leaders need to just accept that, to some extent, resisting potentially difficult situations is normal and natural. Then they need to make sure that these perceptual obstacles *do not* get in the way. Simply anticipate your own hesitations and ambivalence. Tell yourself over and over again that it is okay, and simply move forward and trust the 8-step coaching process to work if you carefully attend to each step.

"To do nothing is in every man's power."
--Samuel Johnson (1709-1784)

3. THE UNDERLYING COACHING EXPERIENCE

What do you want to create?

Before a leader engages an employee in a coaching experience, he/she should decide what experience or mind set is to be created for the employee.

The leader can effectively utilize this coaching session to establish a critical foundation for the employee's experience with coaching--by this we mean the way the employee perceives the coaching experience in terms of key thoughts, emotions, and intentions. Regardless of the topic, agreements, commitments, timetables, etc., the employee will leave the coaching session with new data, opinions, and a frame of mind about the leader. Because leaders benefit from some planning and forethought prior to meeting with the employee, we need to consider the range of responses that may impact the coaching session. The underlying experience falls on a continuum, and an employee may be left at any point between the following extremes, depending on the experience that you create:

content/comfortable_____	challenged/pressured
informed/awakened_____	confused/in the dark
free_____	closed in
confident_____	embarrassed
supported_____	abandoned
empowered_____	scared/frightened
excited/enthused_____	depressed
aware_____	unaware
okay_____	chewed out
feeling accepted_____	feeling rejected
protected_____	exposed
rewarded/encouraged_____	punished
involved in a collaboration_____	manipulated
personally close_____	personally distant
considered_____	offended

CHAPTER 5

THE COACH'S CONTRIBUTION
(winning mental attitude)

The climate of the underlying experience should help guide the discussion style and the way a leader develops a plan of action, offers feedback, seeks commitment, and manages resistance. The process of creating a primary experience requires that the leader put into words his/her intentions and then follow through in a consistent manner as each step is presented. Employees usually remember the quality and nature of their primary experience for longer than the specific topic, actions, or timetables designed to address the particular issue or concern. The employee reaction and interpretation of the experience influence how cooperative and enthusiastic the employee will be in future coaching sessions. The key is to practice putting the intended primary experience into words. For example, if the leader wants the employee enthused about resolving the concern or issue, the leader simply needs to make three good faith efforts to say *it*.

Put your intentions into words

1. "I hope you will really get behind and support the action plan."

2. "Your enthusiasm on this issue will make all the difference in the world."

3. "I hope you leave here feeling as enthusiastic and optimistic as I am."

The bottom line is that if employees understand what the lasting impression is that the leader is trying to create, they will feel less manipulated and more supported.

151

Furthermore, the underlying experience may leave an impression on the employee that will last a long time. The leaders can achieve better results from a coaching session if they will make a conscious choice about how they want to frame and position the main theme of the coaching *experience*.

CHAPTER 5

THE COACH'S CONTRIBUTION
(winning mental attitude)

4. PROACTIVE VS. REACTIVE COACHING

When leaders describe their concerns to us, we can usually divide them into two groups: either the leaders are looking ahead (proactive) and seeking out cues that performance is not meeting expectations, or they are looking backward (reactive) on a difficult situation that has already happened. Both situations require coaching, either to prevent the further development of problems or to correct and salvage what remains from a more critical emergency and prevent future occurrences.

"Don't analyze the wake of the ship."

We contend that it is easier and more effective to engage in preliminary problem solving or exploratory Type-I coaching than it is to do "hard-core" problem solving after behavior is imbedded in time and habit--not to mention the higher emotions involved.   Type-I coaching is good during the early stages of a concern because it focuses on more nondirective information gathering, reaffirmation of plans and commitments, and discussion of potential obstacles.   Type-I coaching has certain advantages in terms of saving money and time, employee learning, and reduced stress on the leader and employee when concerns are handled before they blossom into full-fledged problems.

Type-I coaching

When Type-I coaching doesn't work or when this strategy has been overlooked, then a more intense problem-solving approach will be used. This usually requires a more direct application of all of the coaching skills, including a more direct style of communication.   There is nothing wrong with Type-II coaching: in fact, it is what we

Type-II coaching

usually think of when times are difficult. Type-II coaching simply requires more rigor and completeness of all the steps during the coaching process. If leaders are alert to signs indicating an emerging issue and do not procrastinate, rationalize that the issue is too minor, or excuse the employee because of other positive and offsetting attributes and behaviors, Type-I coaching may alleviate the need for Type-II coaching. A commitment to proactive coaching will help ease the coaching burden and reduce the need for crisis management.

5. COACHING: A *PROCESS* NOT AN *EVENT*

By now the reader will have sensed that coaching is more than sitting down one to one with an employee and discussing issues or concerns. Important preliminary events, like planning and data gathering, are followed by the main event or coaching discussion itself, and then by subsequent events like follow-up and support. It is important to view coaching as a process and not a single event, because people don't change suddenly. Change and improvement in job performance evolve; people like to explore, test out, and pilot new behaviors, plans, or actions. Employees may even want to resist or test your resolve, commitment, or seriousness before they become serious and committed.

There is no question that leaders who are willing to engage in the main coaching event on a regular basis are likely to achieve greater results over time than leaders who do not. Coaching discussion itself provides a focus and a source of accountability that does not occur in the other phases. Unfortunately too many books and training programs seduce you into believing that coaching is as simple as three easy steps, or that it can be done in one minute, or that you can do it by watching 25 short TV episodes of Hollywood actors and then mimicking their actions. These advocates treat coaching as an event, and they don't focus on the dynamics of the coaching process. We feel that by viewing coaching as a process and change as an evolution, leaders will avoid false expectations and impatience won't be built up. All too often we have seen leaders show anger and resentment toward

"Who left this
silver bullet?"

Evolution, not
revolution

155

the employee when change doesn't occur as quickly or completely as the leader would like.

Don't get frustrated-- change takes time

Frustration, anger, and resentment are probably the number one enemies of successful coaching. Unlike a specific event, the beginning and end of a process are ill defined. A leader may become annoyed at the ambiguous structure when he/she considers a "process" view of coaching. A more detailed comparison may be helpful:

	EVENT OR PROCESS			
	Complexity	Structure/ form	Time frame	Change
PROCESS	Issues and concerns are more complex	Steps of the process are cyclical and interactive	Long-run payoff and impact	Steady, deep, and lasting change
EVENT	Issues and concerns are less complex	Steps are linear and sequential	Short-run immediate payoff and impact	Sudden, immediate surface change

Not a one shot effort

Leaders need to think in terms of a series of coaching interventions and plan the content and intensity accordingly. It simply isn't realistic to make coaching a one-shot effort and then relax.

156

CHAPTER 6

POSITIVE MOTIVATIONAL COACHING

A. THE CASE FOR POSITIVE MOTIVATIONAL COACHING

One important point needs clarifying: coaching goes beyond problem solving. Many people misinterpret coaching as only a corrective process aimed at specific errors and deficiencies of an individual. The need for coaching doesn't always have to be driven by problems: challenges, opportunities, and obstacles that transcend any one member of the organization can be the motivating force. This type of coaching is very exciting to do. It is less personalized in nature and therefore not as stressful or tense, although it does require certain skills and characteristics. Many of the same coaching skills, mind set, and approaches that are directly applied to problem solving can be used in positive coaching, designed to empower employees to go farther and contribute in new ways.

Beyond problem solving

Empowering employees

We have found it hard to motivate some leaders to take responsibility for positive coaching seriously. Many leaders tell us, "I don't have any problems with my employees. They are all good people, they work hard and pull their own weight, and frankly I can't think of a thing I would change or talk to them about."

If we had a dollar for every time we have heard this comment, we would be sun tanning in Hawaii rather than writing this book. Managers are trying to tell us that they are "off the hook" because they see nothing to change, correct, or improve upon. They couldn't be further from the truth. In reality, these fortunate leaders need to be as active in

No time to rest

their coaching role as the leader who is beset with enormous problems. In fact, wise leaders will be extremely active when things are going well. They will be coaching and conferring with employees on how to maintain and sustain the current state of affairs or developing strategies on how to move closer to their visions and values. In short, good leaders are not satisfied with acceptable performance. Leaders cannot be silent. To achieve the full potential and maximize employee contributions, leaders need a restless dissatisfaction with the status quo, to encourage others to reach new heights. Whatever you and your unit achieve will be the product of the behavior of those who work for you.

The fact of the matter is organization downsizing, fewer promotional opportunities, career plateaus, increasing numbers of professional employees, and good performers with no specific performance problems are all realities of modern organization life that contribute to the need for positive coaching. Since problem-solving coaching sessions produce a certain amount of stress, it is easy to think that most of the manager's time will be spent in this type of session.

75% of the time will be positive coaching

To put the two types of sessions into proper perspective, managers will spend 75% of their coaching time in positive sessions. The reason we spend a lot of time emphasizing the problem-solving session in our writing and workshops is because this is more challenging, is confronting, and will tax the leader's skills and patience heavily.

158

In the following illustration, the two types of sessions are compared:

Illustration 6.1

	POSITIVE COACHING	PROBLEM-SOLVING COACHING
DEFINITION:	A review of those things the employee is doing well or opportunities for growth and enrichment.	A meeting to plan for improved performance in a specific area.
GOALS:	Increased motivation, growth in the partnership.	Behavior change, correction, and adjustments.
TIME FOCUS:	Future.	Here and now.
LEADERS ROLE:	To understand how to better fulfill and support employee needs and current efforts. To take wise risks and contribute more.	To guide, facilitate, initiate, and manage the problem-solving process. To improve the current situation and help develop a satisfactory direction.

The two types of sessions are different in intent, but the skills and steps of the coaching model apply to both.

The last message the leader wants to send to his or her employees is that they are being neglected or not appreciated, or that their input is not valued. Leaders must understand and act on the fact that employees like to grown, achieve, learn, and develop. Believing that an ideal state of affairs can last forever is sure folly; every organization and employee has room to develop and grow.

Don't neglect them

159

What to do

So what do leaders do? Well, they need to engage the employee in a positive motivational coaching session designed to address these issues of maintenance and further growth in open dialogue. Let us be clear. We are not talking about career growth necessarily, but about growth in the existing job, expansion, creativity, empowerment to contribute more, and job enrichment. The main task of leaders is to communicate to the employee that they are interested, that they recognize a fine effort when they see it, and that they want to know how they and their employee can work together to sustain what they have or to empower the employee to go for a bigger piece of the action. This becomes a powerfully motivating act because, once again, the message is, "I want you to be a partner in the organization." It says that, as leaders, you are interested in the employee's future and making sure everyone is supported with resources and guidance. It reinforces the importance of the employee's needs and that everyone should benefit in the long run. This type of coaching is a strong investment in building a relationship that will last far into the future.

Here's what effective coaches do

From the information that we have collected and the leaders we have observed, we have compiled a list of skills and attitudes possessed by strong positive coaches:

1. They have a clear vision of what they want from their organization. They can articulate their values about the organization and are not afraid to do so.

160

CHAPTER 6

POSITIVE MOTIVATIONAL COACHING

2. They feel as if they can control their future and demonstrate excitement about tackling problems and challenges (restless energy).

3. They know they can't solve all the challenges alone; they value teamwork.

4. They are willing to take intelligent risks and experiment with new approaches (they value creativity).

5. They don't over-control employees, and they give others permission to try out innovative approaches to create ideas and develop their own abilities.

6. They share information and communicate frequently on a one-to-one basis.

7. They accept responsibility for conditions in the group, and they respect the ideas of others (value collaboration).

8. They can describe and articulate the challenges and goals for the group, outline expectations and roles of members, establish timetables for assignments, follow up and maintain accountability, and encourage and reinforce the contributions of others.

The 8 coaching steps that help employees change and improve are very compatible with the attitudes and skills outlined above. Our theory is that if you are an effective problem solver, you can be an effective positive coach. It requires some refocusing, but most importantly, it requires a commitment to invest in this type of relationship.

DEVELOPMENTAL COACHING/ACHIEVING YOUR POTENTIAL

"THE END OF THE LINE"

Use the 8 Steps

We often run the risk of implying that the 8-Step Coaching Model is for corrective coaching only, whereas many leaders and organizations are interested in developmental coaching. In fact, the 8-Step process is equally effective in developmental situations. Let's first talk about what developmental coaching means.

For us, it represents the last frontier of coaching. It is the point at which employees are more fully functional, where you do the final tuning in terms of helping to create completely trustworthy, totally responsible, entrepreneurial partners in your operation. As we see it, you are now doing a type of coaching that encourages the employee to take more and wiser risks, to engage in more self-expression, and to discover what lasting contribution they can make. This is a confidence building process and a creative stage for employees--a chance for them to define a personal mission beyond simple organizational advancement. The beauty of developmental coaching is that it doesn't require advancement and promotion. What you are doing is freeing them up so they can give themselves a "personal" promotion and maximize their self-esteem.

Freeing up the employee

The primary focus of developmental coaching is helping the employee, as well as you, the leader, discover and build toward certain goals:

162

CHAPTER 6

POSITIVE MOTIVATIONAL COACHING

1. A job that has adequate variety, meaning, and usefulness (through a process of informally enriching the employee's work itself).

2. Establishment of a future-oriented mission or set of values and definition of a lasting commitment for the employee.

3. Increased self-expression, creativity, and responsible risk-taking.

4. Sound relationships, integrity, and the sharing of knowledge and skills with others (being honest and authentic).

Goals

You can probably tell by now that developmental coaching is aimed at releasing *all* of your employees potential. It requires that you do certain things:

What to do

A. Trust them more.

B. Give them more responsibility.

C. Defer to them more frequently (judgment).

D. Help them define their values and purpose more clearly (includes inviting employees to express their personal wishes in a dramatic and even radical way so their thoughts can simply be heard and defined).

If this sounds like a set of personal mottoes or a personal policy statement, you are right on track.

E. Let them try some new ideas; give them space to contribute within the rules. Surrender a little control and allow them to act like partners in the business.

F. If others act jealous, then coach them, problem solve, and let them know that it isn't an exclusive club or inner circle reserved for a select few.

Doesn't require a promotion

The challenge for the leader is that many employees do feel stuck. They don't know what to do if they are not moving rapidly in a vertical direction in the company. Your task is to help them achieve their fullest potential right where they are, to get them to look at growth and development in a different way. Many employees will need help to see this opportunity. Culture has taught them that growth, contribution, and satisfaction come only when you are living on "Mahogany Row" or in the organizational stratosphere.

By now you may be feeling some sense of inadequacy as to your ability to help employees find themselves and to discover new ways of contributing to their job and the organization. That is only natural, mainly because all of us are in the same boat as the employees in one way or another. We all could use some positive developmental coaching, and we all wish we had a fully adequate leader who could skillfully help us.

So what do you do? What strategy or approach can be taken with employees who are *not* in need of corrective coaching? The main points have already been covered. You simply need to stick with the steps that have been outlined. Maintain a strong

164

CHAPTER 6

POSITIVE MOTIVATIONAL COACHING

"supportive" stance, as well as initiating action and discussion of the nontraditional opportunities and challenges that lie ahead.

The main thing that changes in your coaching strategy is simply the content of each step, rather than its purpose or intent. The following illustrates the modifications in each step:

How to use the 8 Steps

Step 1: Emphasize collaboration in finding a solution for the challenge. Acknowledge the employee's value and contribution to date. Stress your commitment to the employee's growth and satisfaction. Make necessary resources available as much as possible. Listen, be understanding, and offer support throughout the discussion.

Step 1

Step 2: Present the issue as an opportunity rather than an acute problem. Encourage the employee to express what he/she wants, values, and hopes for. Indicate where things could be done differently and new areas the employee could branch out in.

Step 2

Step 3: Go easy on this step. Simply indicate that while the current situation isn't creating any direct pain for you or the organization, it may create some *future* unrest, boredom, and stagnation for the employee if some changes and initiatives are not *started* now.

Step 3

Step 4: Open up some discussion on ways of challenging the employee or making life at work more interesting and rewarding. Specifically explore some informal job design changes that would give the employee more variety, challenge, and responsibility. Try to

Step 4

165

get the employee involved and participating more. Figure out ways for the employee's knowledge and skills to be shared with others. Help the employee define and articulate a personal mission, policies, and values so he/she can perform and act so as to support them. Determine where the employee might be more creative and innovative, and where some responsible risks could be taken.

Step 5

Step 5: No change here. Ask for a commitment as always!

Step 6

Step 6: Be on the lookout for excuses and resistance because change and some unknowns may be uncomfortable to deal with at first.

Step 7

Step 7: Clarify the future advantages, benefits, and positive consequences of the new direction and action plans.

Step 8

Step 8: Be prepared to follow up. This change will be just as challenging and difficult as correcting a problem. The employee can easily lose sight of what the two of you are trying to achieve. By hanging in there, you are demonstrating your support and commitment. Plan to check on the progress of this experiment after a *very* short period of time. Close with a supportive statement.

CHAPTER 6

POSITIVE MOTIVATIONAL COACHING

C. COACHING THE ABOVE-AVERAGE EMPLOYEE OR OUTSTANDING PERFORMER

One of our biggest fears is that a leader will hesitate to coach strong performers who rarely need to be coached. We, in fact, have the same dilemma in our own organization. We probably could get along quite nicely by smoothing over the small or infrequent issues with these employees. The truth is the above-average employee does, on occasion, create a problem; and they do want developmental coaching. Consequently, the biggest disservice is done to the employee and not to ourselves. These high-achieving employees are trying to tell us indirectly by the quality of their work, that they want to be helpful and *feel* responsible for doing the best possible job.

Everyone needs coaching

You need to approach these employees a bit differently than other employees. In all likelihood, they are knowledgeable, skillful, and self-motivated, and their own personality style probably fits the organization. We find that when a concern or issue develops it results from factors other than those listed above, because this employee wants to work effectively, is talented, and isn't into non-conformity. The only remaining causes of performance problems are perceptual blind spots (the employee made an error and didn't realize it), confusion and misunderstanding (the employee didn't understand that the assignment was his/hers), or inadequate resources (the employee didn't have adequate time, money, equipment, or personnel to do the job). The good news is that these problems are easier to deal with when you

Blind spots

have talented, motivated, and compatible employees on your side. The bad news is that you, as the leader, *must* fulfill your coaching obligation and not allow the employee to blindly plod along thinking all is well on the home front.

Be less directive

We suggest that leaders seriously consider a less directive coaching session with highly talented employees. Since you have so many advantages in your favor, you need merely guide the process using questions and non-aggressive statements, along with a lot of collaboration and support. We can't say this too strongly: the more hard working and sincere the employee, the more you must be prepared to articulate various forms of support during the dialogue so the employee doesn't feel attacked, devalued, and unappreciated. This will prevent the unwanted side effects of a bad coaching session; namely, bitterness and resentment for intruding or over-directing the employee when he/she is very able and willing to act. The employee deserves some credit, and you deserve to know what is happening and how things will be improved or changed in a positive way.

Even good employees don't like to be misled. These people are perceptive; they know when you are being too cautious with them and avoid sticky or unpleasant issues. We simply make the plea to deal with the issues openly, to clarify your intent to work in concert with them.

CHAPTER 7

CONCLUDING THOUGHTS

A. HOW PEOPLE CHANGE

Coaching is a process of helping employees experience and work through the three key phases of change. However, employees don't always need manager assistance in order to change, develop, or improve. Often the employee is perfectly capable of navigating through the key phases of change that result in new behavior patterns and attitudes. For leaders, this represents both good and bad news. The good news is that you will find very few employees who need constant coaching, and the bad news is that you may not be needed as often or as much as you might think.

3 phases of change

Based on our research, we want to describe how people change in organizational and job settings, and how the leader can initiate and support the change process when there is a need.

In the first stage of the change process, the employee is either unaware that change will be useful, or the employee is content with his/her behavior and attitudes. In this stage, the leader is beginning to observe and notice definite signs or early warning signals. With a little time, these observations become more unsettling. Ultimately a decision is reached to either confront the issues or ignore them and just live with the pain and take heavy doses of organizational aspirin; i.e., try to forget it, quit noticing, or rationalize that it really isn't that bad.

1st. stage

The process of guided change moves to stage two when the leader decides to confront and/or the employee doesn't show any signs

2nd. stage

THE COACH

of self-adjustment. In this stage, it is vital that the leader be clear on his/her role. It is easy to adopt a position that, "Hey I'm the boss here. When I tell someone to jump, they better say, 'how high?'" Sorry, this isn't the Marine Corps, and you can't make people change any more than you can make someone be motivated to do a job.

The leader is a catalyst

The leader best serves as a catalyst. This means you can initiate and draw attention to issues. You can help mobilize the forces and ingredients that in turn support and heighten the employee's "felt need" for change, and you can help navigate and adjust the speed of the process. However, the employee will ultimately make a decision to assimilate or resist change. In the Western industrial society, workers should have this freedom.

The leader needs to help facilitate and add clarity when the decisions are tough and unclear for the employees. Ultimately, the employees may be trying to tell you that they are in an incompatible job or relationship match, and they are having difficulty putting this into words. You need to help them explore all the options, even the difficult ones like separation.

Adhere to the 8 steps

Surprise, our recommendation for the leader's role in stage two is to adhere to the 8 steps as a template for the initiating, mobilizing, and guidance of this task. Our belief is that if you trust this process it will work. Stage two is the "main event" for the employees. This is where they come to grips with the issues. Once these issues are laid out, there is usually an initial reaction of denial, excuses, and/or some anger. As the

170

concern is developed the employees will experience tension and readiness for change through introspection and self-analysis. The process presents an excellent opportunity to re-direct the employees to a commitment, new goals and action plans. It can also create a need to re-examine their current level of satisfaction with social relationships, job structure, and career match.

After orchestrating stage two, the leader needs to figure out how to best support the events and activities of stage three. Like learning to play a new sport or a musical instrument, stage three requires some risk taking and a willingness to expose yourself and to be a novice. Remain hopeful even though you feel awkward, uneasy, and self-conscious.

The leader plays a vital role in follow-up encouragement, consultation, and providing tangible help if needed. Once the employee feels a little validation and reward from these initial awkward steps, the new behaviors or attitudes become self-sustaining. The employee begins to feel better, self-esteem rises, and a new state of equilibrium or comfort sets in. This doesn't happen over-night; it takes patience and courage from the leader. You need to give the employee a chance to try, experiment, and fail, if necessary. There has to be some maneuvering room to test and to show room for improvement. Often there is a decline before there is strong detectable improvement.

Our model of guided change gives leaders strong clues about the role they need to play in the three stages. We can't guarantee fast

3rd. stage

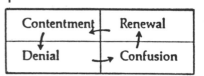

Claes Janssen

Employees need the chance to try, experiment, and fail if necessary.

progress through each stage. We will promise that if you stick with it your chances of having lasting and deep improvement will increase.

3 STAGES OF CHANGE
THE PROCESS OF GUIDED CHANGE

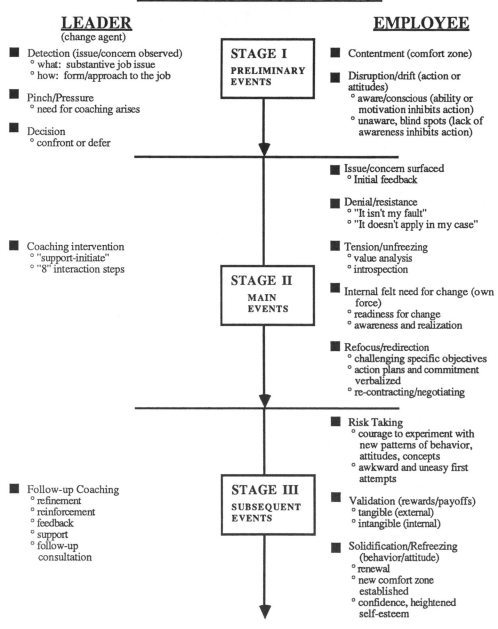

LEADER
(change agent)

■ Detection (issue/concern observed)
  ° what: substantive job issue
  ° how: form/approach to the job

■ Pinch/Pressure
  ° need for coaching arises

■ Decision
  ° confront or defer

■ Coaching intervention
  ° "support-initiate"
  ° "8" interaction steps

■ Follow-up Coaching
  ° refinement
  ° reinforcement
  ° feedback
  ° support
  ° follow-up
    consultation

STAGE I
PRELIMINARY EVENTS

STAGE II
MAIN EVENTS

STAGE III
SUBSEQUENT EVENTS

EMPLOYEE

■ Contentment (comfort zone)

■ Disruption/drift (action or attitudes)
  ° aware/conscious (ability or motivation inhibits action)
  ° unaware, blind spots (lack of awareness inhibits action)

■ Issue/concern surfaced
  ° Initial feedback

■ Denial/resistance
  ° "It isn't my fault"
  ° "It doesn't apply in my case"

■ Tension/unfreezing
  ° value analysis
  ° introspection

■ Internal felt need for change (own force)
  ° readiness for change
  ° awareness and realization

■ Refocus/redirection
  ° challenging specific objectives
  ° action plans and commitment verbalized
  ° re-contracting/negotiating

■ Risk Taking
  ° courage to experiment with new patterns of behavior, attitudes, concepts
  ° awkward and uneasy first attempts

■ Validation (rewards/payoffs)
  ° tangible (external)
  ° intangible (internal)

■ Solidification/Refreezing (behavior/attitude)
  ° renewal
  ° new comfort zone established
  ° confidence, heightened self-esteem

B. 10 BASIC COACHING VALUES

As a result of studying and observing leaders engaged in the coaching process, we have developed a set of basic values inherent to the coaching model. If you have captured the vision of the coaching process, these values will not come as a big surprise. We believe they are worth stating in the hope that more leaders will adopt and assimilate them and that their behavior and actions will be consistent with these values:

Coaching is beneficial

1. *Every employee can benefit* from having access (via coaching) to a leader's wisdom, experience, and unique perspective, regardless of whether coaching involves tough problems, concerns, or positive opportunities for the employee.

Clarity and candor

2. *Clarity* and candor between a leader and employee are fundamental to building trust and respect.

Involvement

3. *Employee involvement* and ownership in developing solutions are vital to the coaching process.

Patience

4. *Patience, planning, and deliberation,* without procrastination, are critical to effective coaching.

Forward-looking

5. Coaching implies a strong, *forward-looking, action* orientation rather than a focus on the past (mistakes, excuses, over-analysis, and fault-finding).

6. *Supportiveness* is the most important ingredient in gaining lasting employee cooperation. There is no substitute for meaningful and serious leader/employee partnerships.

Supportiveness

7. Coaching requires *courage* and *risk taking*. It is never as easy and simple as we would like. Leaders will always feel some doubt and apprehension.

Courage and risk taking

8. *Leaders* and *events play contributing roles* in concerns and challenges facing employees. It isn't healthy to deny these roles. Leaders need to model ownership to their piece of the problem.

Mutual responsibility

9. *Coaching and negotiation aren't always the solution,* but they should be faithfully exhausted before moving on to other management alternatives (i.e., discipline, punishment, separation, etc.)

Coaching isn't the only answer

10. Finally, *trust the process* and attend to the skills and business of coaching that have been outlined in this book. When you neglect or overlook an element, you cut down on your chance of success.

Trust the process

C. IT'S NOT WHAT YOU THINK, COACH, IT'S WHAT YOU DO

**It's all in
the doing**

If you are like the leader or employees in our study, you would have little difficulty describing the elements in an effective coaching session. Even ineffective leaders could correctly define what should occur. The difference was that the ineffective leader was inhibited or could not apply or enact the desired behaviors when asked to do so in a "real time" coaching session. The effective leaders, on the other hand, were able to apply the desired behaviors.

What causes the discrepancy between *knowing* what to do and actually *doing* it? Our best guess is that most managers have the knowledge because they have been exposed to a wide number of good coaching models, both in an organizational setting and off the job--a teacher, minister, friend, professional counselor, etc. Add to this the constant flow of information and literature on effective people skills for leaders. Leaders are also employees, and they know how they would want to be treated by their boss in a coaching session. When you add all of this up, it is not surprising that leaders have adequate sources of informaton to formulate an accurate *mental* picture of quality coaching.

The mystery is why the discrepancy occurs between *descriptions and actions*. One possibility is that, for some, their tough business philosophy of how leaders should *actually* relate to employees is in conflict with the notions of openly exhibiting supportive behavior, seeking employee input, sharing

176

responsibilities for problem solving, etc. This group's values and attitudes about how a manager should relate to an employee get in the way of being an effective coach. Freeing up to apply the positive concepts that they already know requires allowing them to experience the benefits first hand and to see that most employees will not take advantage of them. A behavior change can only follow experimentation with and testing of the impact of the new set of highly beneficial leader behaviors. Furthermore, leaders need opportunities for *extensive practice* in order to become efficient and to convert mental images of coaching into a reality. In a training session, time needs to be devoted to multiple practice sessions in which this experimentation and testing can occur.

You need opportunities to practice

A second possibility for this discrepancy is that some leaders truly believe that their behavior is consistent with their descriptions of an effective coaching session. They perceive no difference between what they say and what they do, even though employees would dispute this. Their problem is more difficult because the managers' perceptions belie the reality of what they actually do as a coach. These managers respond to a presentation of the coaching model described in this text with nods of support. They complain that other managers are incapable of following the model, as they do with their employees. To increase these managers' coaching effectiveness requires their first seeing the difference between what they say and do, then describing what those specific inconsistent behaviors are and the agony they create for the employee. Again, training time needs to be devoted to providing the

Look for differences in what you say and do.

177

managers with candid feedback about their behavior and specific alternative behaviors to experiment with during future practice sessions.

You know what is needed!!

Our conclusion is that managers know what is needed in an effective coaching session. Other than a brief overview and review, we do not need to spend valuable training time telling managers to be more participative or what an effective coaching session entails. We need to spend our time allowing managers to experience the benefits of an effective coaching model and discussing the obstacles to using this model. Second, in providing feedback on their coaching behavior, we need to devote heavy doses of training time to multiple practice and discussion sessions that explore the rewards of good coaching. Our belief and promise are that, if you persist, you will grow increasingly comfortable with the 8-step coaching model and will adapt and incorporate the skills into your own unique style.

D. THE "ART" OF COACHING

Leaders constantly ask us how to be better coaches. Much to their surprise, the answer is short and simple: Be assertive, be realistic, and trust the process. A coach can be helpful to the employee by clearly and directly stating concerns and dealing with important issues; being realistic with expectations, plans, feedback, consequences, and commitments; and trusting the coaching process outlined in this book.

The employee will produce, grow, and become more supportive only if the leader can bring together and orchestrate in a positive way the employee's knowledge, skills, abilities, and willingness to achieve. Leaders don't create this critical mass. The best they can do is highlight, clarify, and serve as a catalyst. The coaching process *does work* if the *employee or manager* allows it to by patiently persisting with the skills and knowledge outlined in this book.

If the employee has made up his/her mind not to change, about the only thing you can try is the ancient art of hypnosis, or else wait until a miracle drug is approved by the Food and Drug Administration. If you will trust the process and pay serious attention to planning, execution of the 8 Steps, and follow-up, you will see some progress. But if it doesn't come early or quickly, please don't abandon the process. A lot of leaders turn back and resort to more drastic measures just when they are on the verge of some progress.

Be **A**ssertive

Realistic

Trust the process

Serve as
a catalyst

E. REGULAR 'T.T.A.' SESSIONS

<u>T</u>alk,

<u>T</u>hink, and

<u>A</u>ct

Frequent contact

Once each week

This is really the essence of Step 8 in the coaching model. . .regular frequent contact. Contact and follow-up are not born out of the need to be snoopy or over-controlling; nor are they an expression of your mistrust of the employee. Rather, they arise from the need to be supportive, interested, involved, and committed, as well as from the need to see results.

At times, when the question comes up (and it does invariably) of how much coaching is enough, the response has been a bit controversial. The hard data on this question suggest ideally once per week (or once every two weeks at the most) if you really hope to gain the benefits of a T.T.A. session. For some leaders with many employees (10 or more reporting *directly*) or for leaders supervising employees with low job task variety or impact, it may be that a monthly T.T.A. session would be very workable. But, frankly, that is as much as we will compromise on answering this tough question. Many managers react quickly and say there are so many other things to do: "I can't afford to spend that much time with employees." Our response is "You're right. . managers will always be busy, and if you believe you are a "leader," as well as a manager, then you can't afford *not* to spend 30-40 minutes in a one-to-one T.T.A. session once each week or two."

CHAPTER 7

CONCLUDING THOUGHTS

The next question or concern that invariably comes up is: "What if there is a lack of issues or concerns to talk about?" We are tempted to say "open your eyes," but that seems a bit curt! Nevertheless, our basic concerns are that you are not attending to "leadership," not delegating enough, not fully utilizing the employee, and not giving enough permission to take some risks or be more expressive. It is you, the leader, who is paying a big price if you are not magnifying your efforts through others or getting the full leverage intended by having employees report to you. If there are no specific concerns or issues, then you can use the meeting time to gather information as an update on progress, do some developmental or motivational coaching, pass along information, etc.. The leader can also ask for feedback, model a positive response to these issues, and show the employee that you are concerned and interested in being an effective partner. Once you have done these things, then give yourself and the employee a break and call the meeting short. In fact, doing this once and awhile is good so employees maintain some freshness and so you respond authentically to the fact that nothing important is happening.

Remember, the important message that you are sending is that this employee and his/her job are as important as budgets, monthly reports, staff meetings, and all the other bureaucratic "B.S." that all leaders and managers have to put up with. We know some initiative on your part will have to be taken to make employees feel important, number one, and to dedicate the time on a *regularly* scheduled basis (i.e., every other

Dedicate a certain time

181

Wednesday) to connect with your employees. We simply find that a lot of organizations either don't want to or don't know how to get leaders to make the employees feel like valued partners and to maintain effective accountability. The system we are proposing is simple, and it takes only a little time. The best way to start is to circulate a memo or post a note that you would like to meet individually with your employees (direct reports) more often and that you have set aside a certain time during the week or month. Once people begin coming in, you can say more about the purpose and intent of the T.T.A. sessions.

CHAPTER 7

CONCLUDING THOUGHTS

F. COACHING VS. PERFORMANCE APPRAISAL

The question often comes up, "Isn't coaching a lot like the familiar performance appraisal process?" Our answer is that it is dramatically different. We originally became interested in the coaching process because of our experiences with the deficiencies of performance appraisal. We had been asked to devise a customized performance appraisal system, along with a training program, for a Fortune 500 corporation. After working through the resistance that naturally accompanies adoption of a massive program such as this, we noticed one consistent piece of feedback coming from managers at all levels. That message was, "Give us some help, ideas, and training on how to manage an employee's performance from day to day, from one concern to the next." These managers grew to accept the performance appraisal process, but they felt that an annual or series of annual performance reviews wasn't the answer to improving employee performance and maximizing cooperation. Something less formal and more flexible was needed to use with employees on a more frequent basis. So we began our preliminary research and data gathering to construct a coaching model or tool to address this very appropriate objection to performance appraisal as the primary management tool for human resources.

Because of this experience, we spend considerable time delineating and defining the differences between these two processes. The following figure throughly differentiates the two methods. We hope it will reduce

"If it looks and smells like a rose, why do we keep calling it a carnation?"

confusion and ambiguity and be useful for those who may be interested in using both processes in their organizations.

COACHING	PERFORMANCE APPRAISAL
DEFINITION	
Interpersonal influence, exercised by a leader in specific situations or in response to *critical incidents or development opportunities,* designed to attain a specific goal or planned change in behavior or attitude. Integrative and interactive communication, dialogue, and exchange are used to gain employee's support for new direction and change.	Formal and more general feedback and information at predetermined intervals designed to apprise employees of the *leader's* perception of job effort and success. To let employees know how they are doing and their relative value to the organization.
GOALS/OUTCOMES	
To take immediate and full advantage of development opportunities as they occur. To have employee understand and accept changes that will increase employee effectiveness. To eliminate obstacles and impediments to better performance.	To provide information for management decision making (rewards, compensation, discipline, promotions, training, succession planning, etc.). To reinforce desired behaviors and objectively evaluate performance over time. To close the books on post performance and plan new goals for the coming year.
TIME FOCUS	
Frequent, as a spontaneous reaction to inadequate behavior or attitudes, or as a regular planned and deliberate "time out." Emphasis on current events, here-and-now concerns and opportunities.	Less frequent (usually annual or semiannual), conducted at the beginning or end of a year or business cycle rather than when work is in progress. Focus on the past and what was or wasn't done.
LEADER'S TASK	
-To confront specific situations or incidents where employee behavior is less than expected or where there is an opportunity for development or learning. -To pose a problem, seek resolution and commitment, integrate ideas, and make agreements and plans.	-To document and evaluate overall strengths and weaknesses. -To review agreements and job responsibilities and to compare against predetermined objectives. -To document the employee's value and contribution to the company and submit performance reports. -To integrate the objectives of the work group and the individual.
VALUES	
Coaching provides an opportunity for the leader to act out and communicate these values: -That it is better to catch problems before they become unmanageable. -That it is wise to aim for modest improvements rather than expect giant changes all at once. -That employees need adequate time to assimilate and demonstrate progress. -That employees need to accept responsibility for change. -That the best results are achieved with a forward-looking/action orientation.	The performance appraisal process seems to value: -General and overall feedback. -Clear documentation and record keeping. -Quantity of topics discussed rather than quality resolutions pertaining to individual events. -A certain amount of secrecy around results and ratings. -Decision making (promotion, salary, training) rather than behavior/attitude change.

CHAPTER 7

CONCLUDING THOUGHTS

G. BEYOND COACHING:

WHEN THINGS GET OUT OF CONTROL

Leaders often ask us, "What do you do when you have tried to coach and counsel an employee about a performance concern and the employee has *not* responded?" Unfortunately we see far too many cases where the leader *hasn't,* in good faith, tried to coach the employee or to put the leader's concerns into words. Oftentimes leaders look for a "quick fix" alternative to what is perceived as a difficult and painful confrontation. We have also learned from first hand experience that coaching is usually not a "one-shot" effort. It may take regular ongoing discussions and experiences to achieve the level of support and cooperation needed.

What if the employee doesn't respond?

When you have truly exhausted your good-faith efforts to coach the employee into a change, you have the right to move to the next best alternative to a coaching-based solution. In certain situations, the employee simply may not appreciate or value the coaching approach. In organizations today, many employees have grown accustomed and dependent on heavy authority in the work place or they just don't feel attached to the job or organization. We are not advocating that the leader wait for someone to pass out a permission slip to try a different approach; rather, the leader should tell the employee that the coaching approach hasn't worked and that it is time to take a different path.

Probably the best thing a leader can do is literally "call time out," pull back, and re-examine the entire interpersonal/working

Other alternatives

contract or agreement with the employee. The leader needs to reconsider the basic assumptions and understanding about the employee's role and terms of employment in the organization. This is a major renegotiation effort. It is very possible that the job demands or personal expectations and objectives of the employee or leader have changed sufficiently that a real pressure point has been created in the leader/employee relationship. Remember, a social contract between a leader and employee works as long as there is "mutual consent and valid consideration" for both parties. If a new agreement and a shared vision of common goals can be reached, then a new state of leader/employee stability and equilibrium will be achieved. If not, the leader and employee should begin to explore and plan a way to separate effectively. Some leaders say they can't get along without the employee. No problem--you simply need to look for creative ways to structure the employee's job or reassign or retrain the employee to cut your losses and limit your exposure. You may consider "down-sizing" the employee's role to fit the needs of the situation.

Disciplinary action

Another strategy is to pursue a path of formal disciplinary or probationary action. Obviously, this is riskier; it may be a path of no return in the sense that cultivating a healthy relationship in a climate of hostility and possibly resentment, anger, and embarrassment over disciplinary action is difficult. You may be forced to pursue this path to the unpleasant end of a separation. . . "the ultimate challenge for any leader." The other thing you may consider is to take two aspirin, grin and bear it, and go on lots of short vacations.

CHAPTER 7

CONCLUDING THOUGHTS

H. IT WORKS IN GROUPS

How many times have you sat in meetings and thought:

> What are we talking about that for?

> What's the point of this discussion?

> We're really getting off track now.

> I don't think they know exactly what they are going to do as a result of this meeting.

> Why make such a big deal over this issue anyway.

Having facilitated meetings; we often make the same kind of observations, and we see a lot of wasted time due to poor meeting management. Managers can hold better meetings by using the 8-Step model as a guideline, especially if it is a problem-solving meeting.

Not another meeting

**How to use
the 8-Steps**

With a little modification, the 8 Steps can be used to improve your next meeting.

Step one

<u>Step One--Be Supportive</u>: As in the coaching session, the meeting leader needs to show support throughout the meeting. This can be done by:

-Encouraging the open expression of differences, disagreements or objections in a way that is not punishing to the person.
-Listening to others point of view
-Accepting some responsibility for the current situation and the issue being discussed.
-Being collaborative/flexible in defining and solving the situation
-Keeping the exchange objective and positive versus subjective, personal, or negative.

There is also a place at the start of the meeting to state your intentions and ground rules for the meeting that indicate your willingness to be supportive and collaborative during the meeting.

Step two

<u>Step Two--Define the Topic and Needs:</u> The leader can help the group crystallize the definition of the situation or opportunities. Write this out on a flip chart, or try to make things as visible as possible. Discuss fully the perceptions of everyone. A consensus on the situation or opportunity can serve as the focal point for all future discussion.

After the definition phase, the members may

want to clarify each other's wants or needs regarding the situation. The idea is not to get a master list but define the similarities and unique differences among the meeting participants. This is an important activity; don't hurry past this step.

Step Three--Establish Impact: The group needs to decide if the current situation or future opportunity is worth doing something about.

Step three

The meeting leader needs to make sure every member has an opportunity to state, agree, or disagree with the list of positive or negative impacts of the current situation. A good question to keep asking the group is, " What effect is this situation having on us?"

Ideas should be captured on a flip chart. In this way, the meeting leader is building a case and has some written support for doing something different. By clarifying the impact, the group is building its own motivation for looking at a new direction.

Step Four--Initiate a Plan: The lessons learned while working with an individual during a coaching session apply directly to groups. Ultimately, the leader wants to know who will do what, when, where, and how.

Step four

In meetings, a lot of good discussion will occur but the action plans are left vague, or the responsibility for implementation is assumed. We suggest that these actions be documented on a flip chart, or have each person write the meeting leader a memo outlining what he/she committed to do as a result of this meeting.

Step five

Step Five--Get A Commitment: This step is simple and is avoided in meetings as much as it is in the individual coaching process. You need to be direct and ask members who are responsible for specific action plans if they are willing to try them. Tie it together, and open the discussion for possible reasons why the agreed-to plans can't be accomplished. Better to know now than later if problems and resistance have set in.

Step six

Step Six--Confront Excuses/ Resistance: Normal excuses can be dealt with by focusing the discussion on what people in the group can control. Keep the conversation forward looking and not focused on the past events that neither you nor the person can do anything about. Be firm; state your belief that something can be done and that with all the intelligence in the meeting something can be figured out. Don't let the meeting get sidetracked discussing excuses.

Some people play the role of a wet towel during a meeting. This is the person(s) who won't move forward, disagrees or argues with every point, doesn't contribute, or is disruptive. The meeting leader needs to bring this behavior out into the open and discuss it as a group. Don't shy away from these people or attempt to ignore their behavior.

Their actions are getting in the way of the meeting being effective. Surface what you see happening and discuss it in the group setting with the people involved; e.g., "We have been talking for an hour and no one has agreed to anything different...(silence)" or, "Every time we get close to a decision, Bob, you start talking about something else."

Step Seven--Clarify Consequences, Don't Punish: The conclusions or actions reached during the meeting represent an opportunity for the leader to reinforce and put into perspective the importance of carrying through with the plans. Be prepared to briefly summarize the benefits of implementing the actions, and ask the group for additional consequences. As in the coaching meeting, make your comments and the time spent on this step fit the needs of the situation don't overdo it.

Step seven

Step Eight--Don't Give Up: The commitments and plans you documented on the flip chart serve as an excellent reference for future meetings. At these meetings post the flip charts and review progress. Initiate problem-solving steps for those areas where the original actions are not meeting the objectives.

Step eight

Many problems or opportunities discussed in a group are more complex than individual problems. The need for follow up is even more critical since many smaller actions must be orchestrated to make for an overall success. We know of no situations where the first meeting was the last. Keep your meetings focused by starting with a review of

Keep your meetings focused

191

the plans and accomplishments to date, and then discuss changes or additions that need to be made.

The 8-step model can help you focus the attention of participants during future meetings, as well as improve the efficiency with which you work through agenda items. The use of a flip chart to document the thoughts leading up to and the conclusions for each of the 8 steps will also help your group stay on track and make the meeting be more effective.

APPENDIX 1

THINKING IT THROUGH--
PLANNING GUIDE

1. Provide some background about this employee.

2. Describe how the employee is creating a concern or problem. (Be specific, descriptive, and nonpunishing...What information do you have?)

3. What will ultimately happen if the employee doesn't change/respond? (Is now the time to get heavy handed or do you want to give the coaching process a chance to work?)

4. What immediate objective or initial solution do you want from the next coaching session? Let the employee be responsible for developing the means to reach the objective.

5. What is your overall long-range goal in working with this employee?

6. Make a list of the reasons why it is to this employee's advantage to change. Circle the three most important ones.

7. Describe your expectations and requirements for this employee in terms of this immediate problem.

8. List statements that express three or four different forms of SUPPORT for this employee.

9. How would you rate:

   a. your level of frustration with this issue
      1_____10
      low   high

   b. your exposure or the impact on you personally if there is no change
      1_____10
      low   high

   c. the level of resistance and conflict that you have experienced in working with this employee
      1_____10
      low   high

If you have two or more scores that are "6" or above, the chances of nonsupportive behavior, aggressiveness, and anger go up. You need to be cautious!

10. Are you able to devote 30 minutes or more, if necessary, to the coaching session? (You run a risk of unfavorable results if you cannot allocate 30 minutes or more.)

APPENDIX 2

TRAINING DESIGN

"All leaders knew what to do. . .however, the best leaders applied it, the others did not."

Having read this far you are probably saturated with information about the coaching process. More reading would fine tune your understanding not build your proficiency--this comes only with practice. You have got to "try it"- not just once, but repeatedly.

There are two good reasons why managers are reluctant to "try it."

1. Experimenting with the 8-Step Model and the supporting skills may carry a higher risk than you're willing to assume. "It feels awkward. What if I don't do it right? How will the employees react? What if I make things worse? I don't have time. We're under too much pressure now to be experimenting." These are typical thoughts that keep managers from trying the concepts and skills.

2. There is not an easy way to judge how you are doing and where improvements are needed. It's like trying to teach yourself how to play tennis--without feedback, you're guessing about what's being done right or wrong.

To overcome these obstacles, readers of this book may want to enroll in our **Coaching and Counseling Seminar For Managers**. The seminar provides an opportunity for managers to:

- participate in a risk-free learning environment that will help clarify the model,
- receive feedback from professionals and peers on how they are doing, and the impact of their behavior.

There is no more efficient way to start becoming the type of partner and coach described in this book than to attend our seminar.

UNIQUENESS OF OUR COACHING AND COUNSELING SEMINAR

We teach managers the "how to's" of being an effective coach in a practical way by:

1. Exploring the subject in great depth.
2. Using questionnaire feedback from employees.
3. Allowing for flexibility in style.
4. Offering post seminar surveys for the manager to measure improvement.
5. Using video examples as an illustration.
6. Addressing both the problem solving and positive motivational coaching discussion.
7. Defining the specific supportive and initiative behaviors for effective coaching.
8. Focusing on skill acquisition, practice, and feedback versus lecture and theory.

PRE-SEMINAR WORK

Before the seminar, participants are asked to complete a questionnaire that assesses their coaching skills, as they see them. Managers also distribute similar questionnaires to their employees for an assessment of the managers' coaching skills from their perspective. These are mailed into the Center For Management and Organization Effectiveness for computer processing. The results are discussed during the seminar and action plans prepared.

LEARNING FOUNDATIONS OF THE SEMINAR

1. Class discussion and practice versus lecture: 60% of the time is spent practicing the concepts and skills. The other 40% of the time is spent presenting the material and discussing questions. Formal lectures are kept to a minimum.

197

2. <u>Practice Sessions:</u> Simulating a coaching sessions does four things:
   a. It allows a specific set of coaching behaviors to be highlighted and practiced.
   b. It allows participants to verbalize and express the skills in a very active yet risk free way.
   c. It provides participants an opportunity to evaluate their own strengths and weaknesses and to receive feedback from others.
   d. It allows participants to practice in depth those skills or concepts they need to work on the most.

The practice sessions are conducted in a setting that is very supportive for the participants. We haven't discovered a better way to develop the participants' proficiencies than realistic role plays.

3. <u>Work groups:</u> Practice sessions are conducted in three-person teams. Each person gets to be a manager, employee, and observer each time. These groups are changed throughout the seminar to provide variation and different perspectives for the participants.

4. <u>Application planning:</u> A final work-group session allows participants to practice the skills and concepts on an actual "back home" situation. This session will help start the transference of the skills learned.

THE SEMINAR

The sixteen (16)-hour seminar can be conducted in any combination of four(4)-hour time blocks. The following is the two-day agenda we use when conducting open, public-enrollment workshops.

DAY ONE

Introductions

Seminar Objectives and Orientation

Introduction to Coaching

A Look at Your Coaching Style

Introduction to the Coaching Model

Lunch

Analyzing your Coaching Style

Behavior Change Strategies

Application of the Coaching Model

Debriefing the Application/Case Study

Questionnaire Feedback

Review and Summary of the Day

DAY TWO

Opening Remarks

The Coaching Model, Steps One, Two, and Three

Case Study

The Coaching Model, Steps Four, Five, and Six

Lunch

Practice Exercise

The Coaching Model, Steps Seven and Eight

Small Group Practice

Applying the Coaching Model Back on the Job

Getting Started on Your Own Change

Discussion, Questions, Seminar Evaluation